100 GRILLING RECIPES YOU CAN'T LIVE WITHOUT

100
GRILLING RECIPES YOU CAN'T LIVE WITHOUT

CHERYL AND BILL JAMISON

THE HARVARD COMMON PRESS | BOSTON, MASSACHUSETTS

The Harvard Common Press
www.harvardcommonpress.com

Printed in the United States of America
Printed on acid-free paper

Library of Congress Cataloging-in-Publication Data

Jamison, Cheryl Alters.
   100 grilling recipes you can't live without / Cheryl and Bill Jamison.
      pages cm
   Hundred grilling recipes you can't live without
   Includes index.
   ISBN 978-1-55832-801-3 (alk. paper)
   1. Barbecuing. 2. Cookbooks. lcgft I. Jamison, Bill. II. Title. III. Title:
Hundred grilling recipes you can't live without.
   TX840.B3A13 2013
   641.7'6--dc23

                                        2012035548

Special bulk-order discounts are available on this and other Harvard Common
Press books. Companies and organizations may purchase books for premiums
or resale, or may arrange a custom edition, by contacting the Marketing Director
at the address above.

Text design by Richard Oriolo
Cover design by Night & Day Design

10 9 8 7 6 5 4 3 2 1

ACKNOWLEDGMENTS

Our gratitude goes out to all you folks who share our passion for fire and flame, meat and heat, pyrotechnics and playing with food—all that is outdoor cooking. After many years, it has been a pleasure to reunite with editor Dan Rosenberg, one of publishing's best. The Harvard Common Press founder Bruce Shaw gave us our early chances to write about this field; he and Adam Salomone, who handle the business side of things at HCP, urged us to return to it. Deborah Durham of Spokespersons Plus Network always has an encouraging word and a good joke, usually at Bill's expense.

We've had the pleasure of grilling on many brands and styles of equipment over several decades. We tested and fine-tuned these recipes predominantly on Ducane Meridian and Viking gas grills, a Twin Eagles Salaman salamander-style gas grill, a Solaire infrared grill, Hasty-Bake and Weber charcoal grills, a Big Green Egg, and a wood-burning outdoor fireplace. Barbara Templeman, Cheryl's partner in an outdoor kitchen and dining design business, insideOUTsantafe, gently prodded us to maintain our focus on recipes appropriate for various settings, situations, and cooking styles.

Thanks to our families and many friends who have found us lacking in hospitality while we worked on this book. You might think that putting together a grill cookbook would be cause for many dinner invitations. The reality is nearly the antithesis of that. While the words and recipes come together, we are hunkered down ignoring just about everyone and everything. Now that the manuscript's turned in and out of our hands, let's get this party started.

CONTENTS

WHY 100 RECIPES?

Because that's how many grilled dinners we cook in a typical year, and we think that's about average for avid grill fans. We like to revisit old favorites on a regular basis, so we don't really need an encyclopedic repertoire. When one of our friends heard the title, she said she'd be thrilled if she had ten things to grill often. If you feel the same, we've got you covered in almost every chapter.

Grilling for friends and family is—or should be—a relaxing and lively way to entertain, and with a good collection of dishes you can feel assured of success. You don't need matching silverware, a seating chart, or even a freshly mowed lawn. Focus on the food to make people feel regally indulged.

Many of the recipes are old favorites of ours, updated and refreshed for this book but based in some cases on dishes we've featured before in other books, magazines, newspapers, and websites. In every instance we've rethought elements of the recipe, tested new approaches, and modified ingredients and instructions accordingly.

Any good book should reflect the voice of its author(s). This one definitely manifests our tastes and perhaps prejudices. We have a particular love of foods and flavors of the Southwest, and think that the traditional practice of grilling fajitas, asadas, and taco fillings works wonderfully. We find kebobs too fiddly for many occasions and feel that the spearing of many things together on a sword is like cooking by committee. We believe that skewered food works best as an appetizer, something to eat while standing. Also, we steadfastly continue to emphasize that grilling, true grilling, is best done over an open flame without using a grill cover. We explain the reasons for that in detail in the following chapter. We don't delve deeply into using wood chunks or chips to add a hint of smoke when grilling because, with such short cooking times, it won't amount to more than a hint at best. When we want real wood resonance, we smoke food slow and low over smoldering wood, the essence of traditional barbecue, and suggest others do the same.

In deciding on our top 100 grill dishes, we each wrote down foods and preparations that we felt had to be included. As you might guess, planked salmon, the superlative ancient technique that's become easily doable at home, was near the top of both lists. It might be a little surprising to some of you, though, that plenty of other fish and seafood appeared on the list of a couple of Rocky Mountain residents. Like most of the country, we can get impeccable quality seafood locally, by putting a little effort into the shopping—and we know that you can, too. The other reason it ranks so highly for us is that, again counter to many assumptions, most seafood can be sizzled over a grill fire as well as or better than by cooking with any other method.

In addition, we grill meaty steaks—rib-eyes and porterhouses and flanks—and hefty chops, as well as burgers galore. We also love fire-seared eggplant, asparagus, and even pineapples and banana splits. We adore pizza on the grill, thinking it to be the closest that you can get at home to top-quality pie short of having your own pizza oven. As a side benefit, pizza on the grill will melt the reserve of your starchiest second cousin faster than the mozzarella, and bring young and old together better than a Willie Nelson concert.

Grill and kitchenware stores, catalogs, and websites are overflowing with devices to hold jalapeños upright, rearrange your ribs, and brand your burgers. We pretty much eschew anything other than a good fire, a spatula, tongs, heatproof mitts, and a small-mesh grill topper for tidbits. Our big exception to avoiding extra equipment is a rotisserie, an old-style device that yielded the expression "done to a turn," keeping the juices flowing throughout the food while getting a good crisp sear on the surface. With today's models, a grill motor takes care of that turning, too, and the cook simply takes a bow at the conclusion of cooking. That's why you'll find a chapter devoted to spit-roasted poultry and meat.

For us, these are our "bucket list" dishes, but we don't wait around to have them once in a lifetime. We return to them frequently throughout the year and urge you to join us. So fire up your grill and let's have a hot time tonight!

100 GRILLING RECIPES YOU CAN'T LIVE WITHOUT

GREAT
GRILL
FLAVOR

The most critical success factor in grilling has nothing to do with whether you cook with charcoal or gas, marinate your food in advance, or serve your meat with a special barbecue sauce. What counts the most is an understanding and appreciation of true grill flavor. That alone can qualify someone as a master griller, regardless of their choice of fuels, the state of their grill, or their skills as a saucier. If you don't have it, you can't even be sure you're really grilling when you cook on a grill.

All methods of cooking, from simmering to frying, produce distinctive tastes and textures, generally more pronounced the better you practice the method. The goal in grilling is to intensify the natural flavor of food through the chemical process of high-heat browning (known in scientific circles as the Maillard reaction). With meat, fish, and poultry, the browning and crisping of the exterior requires direct heat at a relatively high temperature. The fire must be hot enough to shrink the muscle fibers on the surface, which concentrates the flavor, but not so hot that it burns or chars the outside before adequately cooking the inside. When you get it right, the result is a robust amplification of the food's natural flavor along with a scrumptious textural contrast between the crusted surface and the succulent interior. It's an outcome characteristic of true grilling, unlike anything obtained by other outdoor cooking methods except open-flame rotisserie roasting.

The only way to get that special flavor is to fully cook all surface areas of the meat, fish, or poultry over direct heat. That's not difficult to do, but it isn't how many Americans grill. To cook entirely with direct heat requires keeping the grill open rather than covered, just as chefs do in restaurant kitchens. When you cook covered, as many American grill manufacturers recommend, you create an oven effect and do much of the cooking with heat reflecting off the lid. In effect, you are grilling and baking at the same time. The resulting flavor reflects the method, providing a modicum of grilled texture along with a generic baked taste.

Using a cover does simplify the cooking process, particularly for inexperienced cooks, which is one of the main reasons that manufacturers suggest it. You put the food in and leave it there until ready, just like in a standard kitchen oven, and you seldom, if ever, torch your dinner or your eyebrows. With an open grill, you must keep an eye on the food, turn it every few minutes, and move it around as necessary to avoid flare-ups. You must control the intensity of the fire and keep track of time well enough to gauge doneness. Some grill industry promoters say this is just too difficult for the American backyard cook, though it's how people grill at home everywhere else in the world. Personally, we like to be fully involved in the cooking, but even if we didn't, the flavor trade-off would make the little bit of extra effort worthwhile.

Covered cooking on a grill does make sense in stormy weather, and in some cases when you want to bake or roast food outside. Just because you're using a grill in these situations, however, doesn't mean that you're grilling. You can bake a cake in any covered grill that will maintain a steady temperature, but it won't be a grilled cake. We stick with actual grilling in this book except in the chapter on rotisserie roasting, a kindred method of cooking for cuts of meat that are too large to grill.

TIME AND TEMPERATURE

Interviewers constantly ask us about the most common mistake people make in grilling. Our answer sounds strange perhaps, but it's true: We forget that we're cooking. We're enjoying the outdoors, spending time with family and friends, and imbibing our favorite libation. It's easy to neglect the basic correlates of all cooking, time and temperature. To cook anything well in any way, you apply a proper level of heat for the right amount of time. Too often when we're grilling, we don't regulate the intensity of the fire or adjust it appropriately for different foods, and we judge the cooking time on the basis of how long it takes to drink a beer.

That approach works to some extent with forgiving foods such as hamburgers and hot dogs, the first things that most of us grilled. With other ingredients, it's usually a recipe for disaster. We all understand this when we're inside, working in our kitchens. No one would ever try to bake a pie by guessing about a good temperature and then letting it cook until they're ready for dessert. Outside, we want to play looser, but the same principles apply.

Controlling the temperature of the fire is essential. Every food grills best at a particular heat level. The only effective way to measure and then maintain that tem-

HOW HOT IS YOUR FIRE?

To test the intensity of your fire, hold your hand a couple of inches above the cooking grate and count the number of seconds it takes until the heat of the fire forces you to pull away.

- 1 to 2 seconds: high fire
- 3 seconds: medium-high fire
- 4 to 5 seconds: medium fire
- 5 to 6 seconds: medium-low fire

perature on an open grill is the time-honored hand test that people have used for eons in all forms of cooking (see "How Hot Is Your Fire?" on page 5).

You seldom grill meat, fish, or poultry at lower temperatures, though some fruits and vegetables thrive at a reduced range.

The hand test may sound a little primitive for our technological age, but it provides a more accurate and universal gauge of heat than any modern gadget made for a grill. The thermometers built into the hood of many grills register only the oven heat when the cover is closed, not the true grilling temperature right above the fire. In open grilling, the gauges don't measure anything.

Use the hand test on both charcoal and gas fires to establish an appropriate heat level before you begin grilling. Temperature adjustments are simple on gas grills, of course, and not much more difficult on charcoal models. With a charcoal grill, fine-tune the heat level by adding or removing coals, opening or closing vents, or moving the food closer to or farther from the fire, depending on the design of your grill. An adjustable firebox makes the task particularly easy, but even on a standard kettle-style grill, you can rev up or dampen the fire effectively by varying the quantity of charcoal used and the amount of air getting to the coals through the bottom vents.

TWO-LEVEL GRILLING

Thick steaks and a few other foods grill best on a two-level fire, usually starting for a few minutes on high heat and then finishing on medium. On gas grills with three or more burners, you can usually keep a hot fire and a medium fire going simultaneously from the beginning, and on smaller models, you simply turn down the heat at the appropriate point. On charcoal grills, you establish two different cooking areas, one with coals in a single layer for moderate heat and another with coals piled two to three deep for a hot fire.

GAS VS. CHARCOAL

We grill at home with both gas and charcoal, and find little difference in the results most of the time. Unlike their charcoal counterparts, some open gas grills won't get hot enough to properly sear steaks, but they generally work fine with foods that prefer a moderate fire, such as chicken and vegetables. Infrared gas grills and the new propane (LP) models with an infrared burner or searing station possess plenty of firepower for any purpose and offer an even greater temperature range than charcoal.

For us, the choice of fuel is mainly a matter of mood. We choose gas for everyday grilling because of its speed and convenience, and change to charcoal or wood for entertaining to create a more casual, relaxed party atmosphere. We particularly like grilling over a fire built from real wood (not briquettes or charcoal) because it imparts more flavor to what you're cooking. If you don't want to deal with more than one grill, pick the kind that fits you, your purposes, and your budget.

OTHER TIPS AND TRICKS FOR SUCCESSFUL GRILLING

Cooking with the lid open over direct heat, tending your fire, and watching the food and the time—these are the basics of good grilling. There are other important steps toward success, however, that can make a significant difference in your neighborhood renown.

THINK GRATE. Before you put food on a grill, always make sure that the cooking grate is hot, lightly oiled, and clean. Preheat the grate, with the cover down, for up to 15 minutes to get it hot. Raise the cover and measure the temperature above the grate using the hand test (see "How Hot Is Your Fire?" on page 5), adjusting the heat as necessary to the most appropriate level for the food you're grilling. Then carefully brush the grate with a thin coat of oil, applied with a rag or a kitchen brush; don't spray oil on the grill or use excessive amounts that will cause flare-ups. When you're finished cooking, scrape the grate clean with a wire brush before it cools.

READY, SET, GO. Before guests arrive, gather and lay out everything you will need for grilling. Once the cooking starts, you won't have time to scurry around in search of ingredients, tools, towels, or anything else.

TIME THE GRILLING. Calculate how long you expect to be cooking the food, checking a recipe for the information if needed. Then, once you start grilling, set a timer to alert you to turn the food or check it for doneness. We use a small, inexpensive pocket timer available in most kitchen stores.

CHECK FOR DONENESS. If you're grilling a sufficiently large cut of meat, fish, or poultry, use an instant-read meat thermometer to check for doneness, taking care that the probe isn't touching bone. With food that's too thin for a thermometer to register well, such as a boneless chicken breast, cut into the meat when you think it's ready to make sure the center is cooked through.

LONG AND STRONG TOOLS. The only tools you need for grilling—other than a timer and instant-read meat thermometer—are long and strong spatulas and tongs for turning food. Everything else is merely a showman's prop.

CONTROL FLARE-UPS. When dripping fat produces a leaping flame under the food, move your vittles to a different part of the grate, at least temporarily. You don't want burned surfaces. Reduce the odds on flare-ups in advance by maintaining a clean grate, cutting excess fat from meat, and keeping oil in marinades to the minimum needed.

HAPPY-HOUR GRAZING

FIRE-ROASTED OYSTERS WITH TABASCO VINAIGRETTE

To give a tasty uptown twist to a casual happy-hour gathering, nothing is as fancifully different or easier to prepare than grilled oysters. They pop open over the fire, eliminating any need for shucking, and require only a simple dressing to accentuate their briny flavor. Buy a few extra oysters to avoid disappointment if one or more doesn't open. We've never seen them go to waste. **SERVES 4 TO 6**

VINAIGRETTE

1/2 cup plus 1 tablespoon vegetable oil

3 tablespoons distilled white vinegar

1 teaspoon Tabasco sauce, or more to taste

Kosher salt or coarse sea salt to taste

Freshly ground black pepper to taste

2 dozen fresh oysters in their shells, preferably smaller oysters with somewhat flat shells, scrubbed

Several cups of rock salt or a platter's worth of fresh herb sprigs, for serving

1. Fire up the grill, bringing the temperature to high (1 to 2 seconds with the hand test).

2. Whisk together the vinaigrette ingredients in a small bowl.

3. Arrange the oysters in a single layer on the grill grate, deeper shells down. If they don't all fit, place as many on the grill as you can and then add the remaining ones as you remove those that are done. Grill the oysters, uncovered, for 5 to 10 minutes, taking them off with sturdy tongs as quickly as each one pops yawningly open. They burble and sputter a bit as they cook. After 10 minutes, remove any remaining unopened oysters and discard them.

4. Arrange the oysters on one or two big platters, on a bed of rock salt or herb sprigs to hold them upright so they retain their juices. (We leave the open top shells in place for serving so the guests can pop out the oysters with a fork.) Spoon a little of the vinaigrette into each one and offer more on the side. Eat as soon as the shells are cool enough for the guests to handle, slurping as you go. Remind your guests to not eat the rock salt.

GRILLING TIP

For a more robust dish, replace the vinaigrette with a rich barbecue butter. Melt together in a small pan over the grill or stovetop 8 tablespoons (1 stick) butter, 2 tablespoons tomato-based barbecue sauce, a few splashes of Tabasco or other hot pepper sauce, and a couple of good grindings of pepper.

MARGARITA SHRIMP

Nothing tastes better with a margarita than margarita-soused shrimp. Contrary to the conventional wisdom of made-for-TV cooking, we strip shrimp of their shells before grilling them and crank up the heat to high, blistering their tender skin quickly. Don't overcook the shrimp, though, because you will burn the marinade on the surface, spoiling the splendid flavor. **SERVES 6**

MARGARITA MARINADE

1/2 cup tequila

1/4 cup fresh lime juice

3 ounces frozen orange juice concentrate (half of a 6-ounce can), thawed

2 teaspoons vegetable oil

1 1/2 pounds medium shrimp, peeled and, if you wish, deveined

About 30 metal or soaked bamboo skewers

3 large jalapeños, seeded and cut into 8 small pieces each

1 large red bell pepper, seeded and cut into 1/2-inch squares

Kosher salt or coarse sea salt

Minced fresh cilantro, for garnish

Lime wedges, for serving

1. Whisk together the marinade ingredients in a small bowl. Place the shrimp in a plastic bag or shallow dish, pour the marinade over them, and refrigerate for 30 minutes.

2. Fire up the grill, bringing the temperature to high (1 to 2 seconds with the hand test).

3. While the grill heats, drain the shrimp, discarding the marinade. Slide one end of the first shrimp on a skewer, add a piece of jalapeño and bell pepper to rest in the curve of the shrimp, and then slide the other end of the shrimp over the skewer. Repeat on the same skewer with a second shrimp and another jalapeño and bell pepper piece. Assemble the remaining kebobs and sprinkle them lightly with salt.

4. Arrange the skewers on the grill so that the handles angle away from the heat. Grill the kebobs, uncovered, for 1½ to 2 minutes per side, until the shrimp are just firm, opaque, and pink-white, with lightly browned edges. The jalapeño and bell pepper pieces should remain a bit crisp.

5. When done, sprinkle the kebobs lightly with cilantro and serve them hot, with lime wedges for squeezing. As a variation from serving the shrimp on the skewer, we sometimes pile them in margarita glasses with salted rims and lime wedges.

HOT LITTLE NUMBERS FOR GRAZING

Nothing warms up a casual outdoor gathering like hot nibbles from the grill. Served with a cold brew, chilled white or rosé wine, or an iced drink, they draw people together around the food and whet the appetite for more of everything. Each of our choices in this chapter grills quickly and is easy to prep and serve. For other options, consider slices of the pizzas in the following chapter.

You don't need to offer more than one of the starters for a regular dinner party, supplemented perhaps with some olives, an assortment of raw vegetables with a dip, salted nuts, or chips and salsa. On the other hand, you can serve several for a grazing party as a complete meal while your friends stand and chat. Fire up the tidbits and lay them out for guests in two or three successive courses, interspersed with prepared finger food.

SHRIMP RÉMOULADE

Rémoulade may be the happiest culinary marriage of all time in New Orleans, bringing together some of the best seasoning ideas of France and Africa. Apart from the proper balance of creaminess and spice, the key to success is the mayonnaise-like emulsion that requires both room-temperature ingredients and a slow, steady drizzle of the oil to form correctly. Make a little time in your schedule for the shrimp to chill after grilling before you plan to serve them.
SERVES 6

RÉMOULADE

1/2 cup thinly sliced scallions

1/3 cup chopped celery

1/3 cup chopped fresh flat-leaf parsley

1 plump garlic clove, chopped

1 tablespoon fresh lemon juice

1 tablespoon white wine vinegar (tarragon-flavored if available)

1 teaspoon paprika

1 teaspoon salt

1/2 teaspoon prepared horseradish

1/4 teaspoon cayenne pepper

2 large eggs, at room temperature

2/3 cup vegetable oil

1/4 cup Creole mustard or brown mustard

3 tablespoons ketchup

11/2 pounds large shrimp, peeled and, if you wish, deveined

Watercress or other greens, for garnish (optional)

1. Combine the scallions, celery, parsley, garlic, lemon juice, vinegar, paprika, salt, horseradish, cayenne, and eggs in a food processor and blend well. With the machine running, pour the oil in a thin, steady stream through the feed tube. When the oil is incorporated and the sauce is creamy and mayonnaise-like in consistency, stop the machine, add the mustard and ketchup, and pulse to combine. Cover the sauce and chill for at least 45 minutes before serving. (The rémoulade can be made up to 3 days ahead.)

2. Fire up the grill, bringing the temperature to high (1 to 2 seconds with the hand test). Place a well-oiled small-mesh grill rack over the cooking grate.

3. Grill the shrimp on the rack, uncovered, for about 2 minutes per side, turning once. The shrimp are done when just firm, opaque, and pink-white, with a few lightly browned edges. Transfer the shrimp to a dish, cover, and refrigerate until well chilled, about 45 minutes.

4. Use the sauce as a dip for the shrimp, or spoon it over them on individual plates. Garnish with watercress if you wish.

may be the happiest culinary marriage in New Orleans, bringing together some of the best seasoning ideas of France and Africa

SPEARED CHICKEN CAESAR SALAD

Everyone loves a Caesar salad brimming with chicken. It's a classic, but can be a bit boring. This skewered version is bound to delight your friends. Be sure to cut the chicken cubes a bit smaller than the bread so that they cook through before the bread gets overly done. **SERVES 4**

CAESAR DRESSING

1 large egg

1 cup extra-virgin olive oil

1/4 cup fresh lemon juice

1/2 teaspoon Worcestershire sauce

2 garlic cloves, minced

Kosher salt or coarse sea salt

Freshly ground black pepper

1 pound boneless, skinless chicken breasts, cut into 3/4- to 1-inch cubes

4 ounces country bread, cut into 1- to 11/4-inch cubes

2 to 3 tablespoons garlic-flavored olive oil or top-quality extra-virgin olive oil

4 metal or soaked bamboo skewers

8 cups romaine ribbons or a similar quantity of crisp whole romaine leaves

Freshly ground black pepper

Curls of Parmigiano-Reggiano (made with a vegetable peeler scraped over the cheese), for garnish

1. To prepare the dressing, first bring about 3 inches of water to a boil in a small sauce-pan. Slip the whole egg into the water, boil (or "coddle") for exactly 1 minute, and remove from the heat. Pour the oil into a small bowl. Crack the egg (which will be vis-

cous but still runny) into the oil and whisk until combined. Whisk in the lemon juice, Worcestershire, and garlic until the mixture is emulsified and thick. Season with salt and pepper to taste. (The dressing can be made up to 1 day ahead; store it covered in the refrigerator.)

2. Place the chicken cubes in a zipper-top plastic bag. Pour 1/2 cup of the dressing over the chicken, reserving the rest in the refrigerator. Seal the bag, toss back and forth to coat the chicken, and refrigerate for at least 1 hour and up to 4 hours.

3. Drain the chicken, discarding the marinade, and let it sit, uncovered, at room temperature for about 20 minutes.

4. Fire up the grill, bringing the temperature to medium (4 to 5 seconds with the hand test).

5. Brush the bread cubes with the garlic oil, and skewer them more or less alternately with the chicken cubes.

6. Arrange the skewers on the grill so that the handles angle away from the heat. Grill, uncovered, for 7 to 9 minutes, turning to cook on all sides, until the chicken is firm and white but still juicy. The bread will get toasty brown.

7. Toss the romaine with enough of the remaining dressing to moisten it thoroughly, then divide the lettuce among four plates. Place a chicken-bread skewer on each plate. Sprinkle with pepper to taste, garnish with cheese curls, and serve while the chicken is still hot and the romaine is still cold.

SUBLIME SALBUTES

One of the most beloved dishes of the Yucatan, a *salbute* combines juicy shredded chicken and orange-pickled onions on crunchy tostadas. A marinade featuring the local achiote paste—easy to find these days in most American supermarkets and Latino grocery stores—produces a deep mahogany crust on the grilled chicken. **SERVES 4**

ORANGE-PICKLED ONIONS

1 medium-size red onion, sliced into thin rings

1/2 cup red wine vinegar

3 ounces frozen orange juice concentrate (half of a 6-ounce can), thawed

1/2 teaspoon dried oregano, preferably Mexican

ACHIOTE MARINADE

1/4 cup cider vinegar

3 ounces frozen orange juice concentrate (half of a 6-ounce can), thawed

1 tablespoon achiote paste

3 garlic cloves, minced

2 teaspoons dried oregano, preferably Mexican

1 bay leaf, crumbled

1/2 teaspoon ground allspice

Two 6-ounce boneless, skinless chicken breast halves, pounded to 1/2-inch thickness

Kosher salt or coarse sea salt

Freshly ground black pepper

4 tostada shells (flat fried taco shells) or a dozen or more large tortilla chips

Minced fresh cilantro, for garnish

1. At least 1 day and up to 3 weeks before you plan to serve the *salbutes*, place the onion slices in a medium-size bowl. Pour enough hot water over the onions to cover them by about 1 inch. Let the onions soak for 10 minutes to eliminate the strong flavor, then drain off the water. Stir the remaining ingredients into the onions, cover, and refrigerate for at least 24 hours. (This makes enough onions for a couple of batches of chicken and tostadas. Leftover onions make a great accompaniment to almost any grilled sandwich or quesadilla.)

2. At least 1 hour and up to 4 hours before you plan to grill the chicken, whisk together the marinade ingredients in a small bowl. Place the chicken in a zipper-top plastic bag or shallow dish, pour the marinade over it, and refrigerate.

3. Fire up the grill, bringing the temperature to medium (4 to 5 seconds with the hand test).

4. Drain the chicken, discarding the marinade, and place it on a plate. Sprinkle the chicken lightly with salt and pepper, and let it sit, covered, at room temperature for about 20 minutes.

5. Grill the chicken, uncovered, for 5 to 6 minutes per side, until opaque but still juicy. (The chicken can be prepared to this point up to 2 days ahead and kept covered and refrigerated. Reheat wrapped in foil in a low to medium oven or covered grill.)

6. Shred the warm chicken and toss it with 1 to 2 tablespoons of the onion pickling liquid. Pile equal portions of chicken on each tostada shell, top with a generous tangle of pickled onions and a sprinkling of cilantro, and serve immediately.

MOROCCAN CHICKEN WINGS

They don't know what they're missing in Buffalo. This rendition of the city's most popular snack soars sensuously into heavenly realms with help from harissa, Morocco's signature chili paste, sold widely in supermarkets and in Middle Eastern groceries in tubes or small jars. If you can't find it, though, substitute a similar quantity of an Asian chili-garlic paste. **SERVES 4 TO 6**

HARISSA MARINADE
1/2 cup extra-virgin olive oil

1/4 cup fresh lemon juice

2 tablespoons harissa, or more to taste

1 teaspoon packed brown sugar

1 teaspoon ground cinnamon

1 teaspoon kosher salt or coarse sea salt

2 3/4 to 3 pounds chicken wings or 2 1/2 to 2 3/4 pounds wing drumettes

1 1/2 tablespoons minced fresh mint

1 1/2 tablespoons minced fresh cilantro

1. Whisk together the marinade ingredients in a bowl. Set aside about one-third of the marinade to use for basting.

2. With a cleaver or other large knife, remove the bony tips from the wing ends. Then cut each wing in half at the joint. (If using wing drumettes, no cutting is needed.) Place the wing sections in a large zipper-top plastic bag and pour the larger portion of the marinade over them. Seal the bag and toss back and forth to coat the wings evenly. Refrigerate for at least several hours and preferably overnight.

3. Fire up the grill, bringing the temperature to medium (4 to 5 seconds with the hand test).

4. Mix the reserved marinade with the mint and cilantro.

5. Grill the chicken wings, uncovered, for 4 to 5 minutes, turning to sear on all sides, then turn and brush occasionally with the reserved marinade for another 5 minutes. Let cook for a final 3 to 4 minutes without basting so that the surface crisps up a bit. When done, the chicken should be cooked through, with the sauce charred lightly in a few spots and chewy in others. Serve warm, piled high on a colorful platter to eat as finger food.

soars sensuously into heavenly realms with help from harissa, Morocco's signature chili paste

SASSY SATAY

Originally from Indonesia, satay has become a world traveler, now known in every corner of the globe and altered incrementally over time by its contact with different cultures. Our classic satay dip for this feast of chicken and pork stays close to its Asian roots, but we also add a second, totally nontraditional sauce. If you wish, substitute more of one meat for the other, or cut the prep time by making just one of the sauces, simply doubling the quantity. **SERVES 4 TO 6**

CLASSIC SATAY SAUCE

1 tablespoon peanut oil

3 tablespoons minced onion

2 plump garlic cloves, minced

1 cup unsweetened coconut milk (not cream of coconut)

1/2 cup creamy peanut butter

1 1/2 tablespoons Asian fish sauce

1 1/2 tablespoons packed brown sugar

3/4 teaspoon curry powder

One 2-inch cinnamon stick

1 bay leaf

Grated zest and juice of 1 lime

FIRE-AND-ICE SAUCE

1 cup plain yogurt

1 jalapeño, seeded and minced

1/3 cup minced fresh cilantro

1/3 cup minced fresh mint

MARINADE

6 tablespoons granulated sugar

1/4 cup Asian fish sauce

2 tablespoons peanut oil

Juice of 1 lime

1 teaspoon curry powder

1 pound boneless, skinless chicken breasts, sliced across the grain into $1/2$-inch-thick strips

1 pound pork loin, sliced across the grain into $1/2$-inch-thick strips

About 30 metal or soaked bamboo skewers

1. To make the satay sauce, first warm the oil over medium-low heat in a large, heavy saucepan. Cook the onion and garlic until very soft, about 10 minutes, lowering the heat further if any edges begin to brown. Stir in the rest of the sauce ingredients and raise the temperature to medium. Simmer the sauce for 25 to 30 minutes, stirring occasionally at first and more often as it thickens. Remove the cinnamon stick and bay leaf. For a smoother sauce, puree in a blender before serving. (The satay sauce can be made several days ahead and kept covered and refrigerated. Reheat or bring back to room temperature before serving. Add a little water if the sauce is too stiff for dunking.)

2. Combine the fire-and-ice sauce ingredients in a small bowl. Cover and refrigerate until needed. (The sauce can be made several hours ahead of serving.)

3. To make the marinade, stir together the sugar and fish sauce in a small, heavy saucepan. Melt the mixture over medium-low heat, stirring occasionally, and continue cooking for a few minutes until it forms a thick, bubbling syrup. Remove the pan from the heat and immediately stir in the oil, lime juice (watch out for the steam), and curry powder. While you allow the marinade to cool for a few minutes, place the chicken and pork strips in separate zipper-top plastic bags or shallow dishes. Spoon equal amounts of the thick, caramelized marinade over the chicken and pork, rub it thoroughly over all the strips, and refrigerate for 30 to 60 minutes.

4. Fire up the grill, bringing the temperature to medium (4 to 5 seconds with the hand test). While the grill heats, drain the chicken and pork strips, discarding the marinade, and thread each strip onto a skewer.

5. Arrange the skewers on the grill so that the handles angle away from the heat. Grill the skewered strips, uncovered, for 4 to 5 minutes, turning at least once.

6. Serve the skewers hot off the grill with the two sauces.

LETTUCE WRAPS WITH ASIAN STEAK

Everyone loves lettuce wraps—ubiquitous these days on upscale restaurant menus—and they provide a good way to involve your guests in assembling the meal. They even work as a main course, if you prefer, served four to six per guest with steaming white rice or long egg noodles and some store-bought Asian peanut or ginger sauce. Flank steak is a terrific meat for the grill because its breadth offers lots of surface to be seared by the fire. **SERVES 4 TO 6**

MARINADE

3/4 cup soy sauce

1/4 cup rice vinegar

2 1/2 tablespoons sugar

2 tablespoons minced fresh ginger

1 tablespoon Asian toasted sesame oil

1 teaspoon Korean or other Asian chili paste, or more to taste

3 garlic cloves, minced

3 scallions, roots and limp tops trimmed, chopped

One 1 1/2-pound flank steak

1 small red onion (optional), sliced into thin half-rings

3 tablespoons fresh lime juice (optional)

About 2 dozen crisp butter, Bibb, or romaine lettuce leaves

2 tablespoons sesame seeds, toasted in a dry skillet over medium heat until fragrant

1. Whisk together the marinade ingredients in a small bowl. Set aside about one-quarter of the marinade to use for serving. Place the steak in a zipper-top plastic bag and pour the larger portion of marinade over it. Seal the bag and toss back and forth to

distribute the marinade. Let sit at room temperature for 30 minutes while you prepare the grill.

2. Fire up the grill, bringing the temperature to high (1 to 2 seconds with the hand test).

3. Drain the steak, discarding this portion of the marinade. Grill the steak, uncovered, for 3 to 4 minutes per side, until well seared on the surface but still pink at the center.

4. Let the steak sit for 5 minutes. Meanwhile, in a small bowl toss together the onion and lime juice, if you wish. Slice the steak across the grain into strips no more than 1/4 inch thick. Cut the strips into thirds. Toss the steak with the reserved marinade and arrange on a platter. Accompany with a plate of lettuce leaves, the optional onion mixture, and the toasted sesame seeds.

5. To assemble, let guests spoon about 1/4 cup of the steak onto each lettuce leaf. Top with onion, if you wish, and sprinkle with sesame seeds. Fold the mixture up, somewhat taco-like, to enjoy.

a good way to involve your guests in assembling the meal

GRILLED CHEESE SANDWICH ON A STICK

A grilled cheese sandwich is usually cooked on a griddle rather than a grill, but we decided to take the name literally. The result is equally wonderful and better suited to an outdoor gathering. Just pick a proper cheese that won't melt all over your grate, like halloumi from Cyprus or panela from Mexico, both of which hold their shape when warmed. **SERVES 4 TO 6**

> 1 pound halloumi, panela, or ricotta salata cheese, cut into 1- to 1¼-inch cubes, at room temperature
>
> 4 ounces country bread, cut into 1- to 1¼-inch cubes
>
> 1 lemon, cut into ½-inch-thick rounds and each round cut into quarters
>
> 12 metal or soaked bamboo skewers, preferably 9 to 10 inches long
>
> Several tablespoons garlic-flavored olive oil or top-quality extra-virgin olive oil
>
> Sweet or hot paprika

1. Fire up the grill, bringing the temperature to medium (4 to 5 seconds with the hand test).

2. Slide one cheese cube, one bread cube, and one lemon chunk onto each skewer. Repeat with a second trio of cubes on each skewer. Brush the kebobs with the olive oil.

3. Arrange the skewers on the grill so that the handles angle away from the fire. Grill, uncovered, for 5 to 7 minutes, turning on all sides, until the bread is toasty and the cheese is browned in spots and soft. Transfer to small plates or a platter, sprinkle paprika over the top, and serve immediately.

GOAT CHEESE WRAPPED IN GRAPE LEAVES

For a combination of earthy presentation and elegant flavor, hardly anything beats softened, tangy goat cheese served in charred grape leaves. For us, it's a definite top 100 go-to dish for almost any occasion. **SERVES 4 TO 6**

4 to 6 large grape leaves, blanched if fresh or rinsed if bottled

One 5- to 7-ounce round or log fresh goat cheese

2 teaspoons extra-virgin olive oil

1 tablespoon minced fresh herbs, such as chives, oregano, or thyme (optional)

Diced tomato, caper berries, and briny green or black olives, for serving

Crackers or small toasts, for serving

1. Arrange the grape leaves more or less in a circle, overlapping the leaves enough to cover any holes. You want a solid wrapper of leaves. Place the cheese in the center of the leaves. Pour 1 teaspoon of the oil over the cheese and sprinkle with the herbs if you like. Wrap the leaves up over the cheese, covering it completely. The leaves will adhere to the cheese. Coat the leaves with the remaining 1 teaspoon oil.

2. Fire up the grill, bringing the temperature to medium (4 to 5 seconds with the hand test).

3. Grill the packet, uncovered, for 6 to 8 minutes, turning on all sides, until the cheese is soft but short of oozing out of the protective wrap of semi-charred leaves.

4. Transfer the cheese to a platter. Fold the grape leaves back from the top of the cheese. Scatter the tomato, caper berries, and olives around the cheese and fill the remaining portion of the platter with crackers or toasts.

ANTIPASTO EXTRAVAGANZA

This is as simple as it gets. Just bathe these (or other) seasonal vegetables in a basic vinaigrette, grill them a couple of hours before you want to eat, and top them with a tomato relish at the last minute. You can even skip the relish if you like, instead drizzling a bit more good olive oil over the platter before serving. If you've never tried an especially coarse and flaky salt, such as Maldon sea salt, give it a go here. It looks beautiful and the taste is a revelation. **SERVES 4 TO 6**

VINAIGRETTE

1/2 cup plus 1 tablespoon extra-virgin olive oil

3 tablespoons white wine vinegar

1 garlic clove, minced

1/4 teaspoon Dijon mustard

Kosher salt or coarse sea salt to taste

Freshly ground black pepper to taste

About 8 metal or soaked bamboo skewers (optional)

1 large red onion, sliced into 1/2-inch-thick rings

1 large red, orange, or yellow bell pepper

1 eggplant (about 1 pound), sliced into 1/3- to 1/2-inch-thick rounds

2 to 3 small heads radicchio, quartered through the stem end, or 4 to 6 endives, halved through the stem end

1 small fennel bulb, trimmed and cut into 1/3- to 1/2-inch-thick slices through the stem end

1 zucchini (about 1/2 pound), cut into 1/3- to 1/2-inch-thick slices

2 to 3 red-ripe plum tomatoes, halved lengthwise

RELISH

2 red-ripe plum tomatoes, finely diced

2 tablespoons minced fresh basil or flat-leaf parsley

1 tablespoon top-quality extra-virgin olive oil

Flaky sea salt (such as Maldon), kosher salt, or coarse sea salt

Capers, caper berries, green or black olives, or Parmigiano-Reggiano curls (made with a vegetable peeler), for garnish (optional)

1. Whisk together the vinaigrette ingredients in a small bowl. Set aside about one-quarter of the vinaigrette to use for basting.

2. If you wish, run a skewer through each onion slice to hold the rings together while cooking. Brush the vegetables with the remaining vinaigrette, giving the eggplant slices the heaviest coat.

3. Fire up the grill, bringing the temperature to medium (4 to 5 seconds with the hand test).

4. Grill the vegetables, uncovered, in batches if necessary. Plan on grilling times of 12 to 15 minutes for the onion slices and whole bell pepper; 8 to 12 minutes for the eggplant, radicchio, and fennel bulb; 6 to 8 minutes for the zucchini; and 4 to 6 minutes for the tomatoes. Arrange the tomatoes cut sides down first. Turn the pepper on all sides to cook evenly, and the rest of the vegetables three times, brushing with the reserved vinaigrette as they cook. Cook until tender, removing each vegetable as it is done.

5. As soon as the pepper is done, transfer it to a plastic or paper bag, close, and let it steam until cool enough to handle. Pull the charred loose skin from the pepper. Slice the pepper into thin strips, discarding the seeds and stem.

6. Arrange the vegetables attractively on a platter. Serve warm or at room temperature. Just before serving, stir together the tomato relish. Top the vegetables with the relish, a sprinkling of salt, and any of the optional garnishes.

GRILLING TIP

Transform the antipasto into a full vegetarian meal by layering the vegetables over crusty grilled polenta on individual plates, with a portion of the relish dabbed on each.

PARTY-TIME PIZZAS

CLASSIC ITALIAN PIZZA WITH FIRE-ROASTED TOMATO SAUCE

In 1889, according to pizza lore, Queen Margherita of Italy paid her first visit to Naples, the original home of pizza. A local baker prepared a special pie in her honor, one flaunting the colors of the nation's flag: red (tomato), white (mozzarella), and green (basil). This version is still called a Margherita today, and it remains the prototype for all other styles of Neapolitan pizza, which consistently boast a wonderfully thin and crispy crust and a relatively light coat of toppings. This minimalist style works great on a grill, which emulates the high-fire cooking process of a wood-burning pizza oven. If you make a thicker crust or load it with too many goodies, a grilled pie gets soggy and becomes difficult to maneuver and eat. This recipe doubles up on the grilled flavor with a homemade sauce of fire-charred tomatoes, but you can substitute a light coating of any other pizza sauce, if you wish. **MAKES TWO 11-INCH PIZZAS**

FIRE-ROASTED TOMATO SAUCE

3 red-ripe plum tomatoes

2 tablespoons tomato paste

2 tablespoons chopped fresh basil

1 tablespoon top-quality extra-virgin olive oil

Splash or two of garlic-flavored olive oil (optional)

Kosher salt or coarse sea salt to taste

6 ounces fresh mozzarella, sliced and blotted of moisture, or burrata, torn into thumbnail-size bits, or 1¼ cups grated mozzarella

Pinch or two of crushed red pepper (optional)

½ cup lightly packed thin-sliced fresh basil

Primo Pizza Dough for the Grill (page 36)

1. Fire up the grill for a two-level fire capable of cooking at the same time on both high heat (1 to 2 seconds with the hand test) and medium-low heat (5 to 6 seconds with the hand test); see page 6.

2. Grill the tomatoes over high heat, uncovered, for 6 to 8 minutes, turning on all sides, until the skins are somewhat blackened and split and the tomatoes are soft. As soon as the tomatoes are cool enough to handle, halve them and squeeze out the watery liquid. Puree the tomatoes in a blender or food processor with the remaining sauce ingredients.

3. Place the tomato sauce, mozzarella, red pepper (if using), basil, and a spoon within easy reach of the grill. The process must go quickly once you begin cooking. Place a baking sheet on a convenient work surface near the grill and have a large spatula or pizza peel handy.

4. Place the first crust on the grill, laying it directly on the cooking grate over high heat. Grill, uncovered, for 1 to 1$1/2$ minutes, until the crust becomes firm but is still flexible. Don't worry about any bubbles that form on the crust as they will be flattened when you turn over the crust in the next step.

5. Using the spatula or peel, flip the crust onto the baking sheet, cooked side up. Immediately spoon on half of the tomato sauce, and sprinkle with half of the cheese and, if you wish, a bit of red pepper. Quickly return the pizza to the grill (without the baking sheet), uncooked side down. Arrange the pie so that half of it is over high heat and the other half is over medium-low. Cook the pizza for another 3 to 4 minutes, rotating it in quarter turns every 30 to 45 seconds. This may sound awkward but becomes second nature very quickly. Using the spatula to lift the edge slightly, check the bottom during the last minute or two, rotating a bit faster or slower if needed to get a uniformly brown, crisp crust. Scatter the basil over the top shortly before removing the pizza from the grill.

6. Slice the pizza into wedges and serve immediately. Repeat the process for your second pizza.

PRIMO PIZZA DOUGH FOR THE GRILL

The crust for a grilled pizza should be a supporting player of importance, not just a lackluster base for a pile of toppings. You can use a store-bought crust, but we've yet to find one that gives us the crispy, crunchy, flavorsome results that come from this homemade dough, which is a little stiffer than average.

MAKES TWO THIN 11-INCH PIZZA CRUSTS

2 cups flour, preferably bread flour, or unbleached all-purpose flour (or more if needed)

3 tablespoons cornmeal, preferably coarse ground

1 teaspoon salt

1 teaspoon rapid-rise yeast

3/4 cup lukewarm water, 105° to 115°F

2 tablespoons plus 1 teaspoon extra-virgin olive oil

1. In a food processor, pulse together the flour, cornmeal, salt, and yeast. With the motor running, add the water and 2 tablespoons of the oil. Continue processing for about 30 seconds more, until the dough forms a fairly cohesive ball that is smooth and elastic. If it remains sticky, add another tablespoon or two of flour.

2. Knead the dough a few times on a floured work surface, forming it into a ball. Pour the remaining 1 teaspoon oil into a large bowl and add the dough, turning it around and over until coated with oil. Cover with a damp cloth. Set the dough in a warm, draft-free spot and let it rise until doubled in volume, about 1 hour.

3. Punch down the dough on a floured surface, and let it rest for 10 minutes. Form the dough into two thin disks, each about 1/8-inch-thick and 11 inches in diameter. We find a combination of first flattening the crust with a rolling pin and then stretching and prodding it with fingers works best. (A raised edge isn't necessary.)

The dough is ready to use at this point, or can be saved for later in the refrigerator or freezer. Line a baking sheet with wax paper and stack the crusts on it, with another sheet of wax paper between the crusts. Chill the crusts on the baking sheet for about 30 minutes to firm the dough, then remove from the baking sheet and wrap the crusts in plastic wrap before storing. Refrigerate for up to 3 days, or freeze for up to 1 month. Bring the crusts back to room temperature before proceeding.

GRILLING TIP

To personalize your pizza, consider some of these additional toppings, but don't load up the pie with too much of a good thing.

- capers or sliced large caper berries, perhaps with minced anchovies

- green and black olives or drizzles of tapenade

- sliced grilled octopus or calamari

- sautéed wild mushrooms (this is especially good if you include some roasted garlic)

- red-ripe plum tomato slices, blotted of moisture

- fresh arugula, or sautéed escarole or radicchio

Use mozzarella or tomato sauce as a base, or simply scatter the topping alone on the crust.

CLAM AND SAUSAGE PIZZA

In contrast to the few fresh, local ingredients favored as pizza toppings in southern Italy, Americans sometimes pile on a cartful of groceries, including tomato sauce, sausage, pepperoni, pineapple, bell peppers, mushrooms, and much more. In a nod to both traditions, this pizza features a bounty of flavors but keeps the toppings in balance with the crust underneath. Clams and pork are a natural match. **MAKES TWO 11-INCH PIZZAS**

SHALLOT AND VERMOUTH SAUCE

3 tablespoons top-quality extra-virgin olive oil

3 tablespoons minced shallots

1/2 cup dry vermouth

1/4 cup bottled clam juice or seafood stock

1 small red-ripe plum tomato, chopped

CHEESE TOPPING

3/4 cup grated mozzarella, at room temperature

1/2 cup freshly grated Parmigiano-Reggiano, at room temperature

1 garlic clove, minced

1/2 to 1 teaspoon crushed red pepper

1/2 teaspoon dried oregano

1/2 teaspoon dried thyme

Two 4- to 5-ounce sweet or hot Italian sausage links, grilled or otherwise cooked and sliced thin, still warm

3/4 cup shelled cooked small clams, such as littlenecks, or mussels, still warm

1/4 cup minced fresh flat-leaf parsley

Primo Pizza Dough for the Grill (page 36)

1. To prepare the sauce, first warm the oil in a small skillet over medium heat. Stir in the shallots and sauté them for several minutes until very soft. Pour in the vermouth and clam juice, add the tomato, and raise the heat to medium-high. Boil the sauce briefly, until reduced to about 6 tablespoons; remove from the heat and set aside.

2. Fire up the grill for a two-level fire capable of cooking at the same time on both high heat (1 to 2 seconds with the hand test) and medium-low heat (5 to 6 seconds with the hand test); see page 6.

3. Combine the cheese topping ingredients in a medium-size bowl.

4. Place the cheese mixture, sauce, sausage, clams, parsley, and a spoon within easy reach of the grill. The process must go quickly once you begin cooking. Place a baking sheet on a convenient work surface near the grill and have a large spatula or pizza peel handy.

5. Place the first crust on the grill, laying it directly on the cooking grate over high heat. Grill, uncovered, for 1 to 1½ minutes, until the crust becomes firm but is still flexible. Don't worry about any bubbles that form on the crust as they will be flattened when you turn over the crust in the next step.

6. Using the spatula or peel, flip the crust onto the baking sheet, cooked side up. Immediately spoon on half of the sauce, sprinkle with half of the cheese mixture, and top with half of the sausage, clams, and parsley. Quickly return the pizza to the grill (without the baking sheet), uncooked side down. Arrange the pie so that half of it is over high heat and the other half is over medium-low. Cook the pizza for another 3 to 4 minutes, rotating it in quarter turns every 30 to 45 seconds. This may sound awkward but becomes second nature very quickly. Using the spatula to lift the edge slightly, check the bottom during the last minute or two, rotating a bit faster or slower if needed to get a uniformly brown, crisp crust.

7. Slice the pizza into wedges and serve immediately. Repeat the process for your second pizza.

HOT AND COOL PIZZA

A hot crust, bubbling with melted cheese, mates here with a cold and tangy salad topping. For triple-play pizzazz, serve the pizza with a crisp, dry rosé wine. **MAKES TWO 11-INCH PIZZAS**

SALAD TOPPING

3 cups arugula or watercress, any gangly stems pinched off

2 small red-ripe plum tomatoes, chopped

1/4 cup diced red onion, soaked for several minutes in hot water and drained

1/4 cup small capers, rinsed if you prefer a milder flavor

1 tablespoon extra-virgin olive oil

1 to 2 splashes of red wine vinegar

CHEESE TOPPING

3/4 cup grated mozzarella, at room temperature

1/2 cup freshly grated Parmigiano-Reggiano, at room temperature

2 tablespoons minced fresh basil

1 garlic clove, minced

1/2 teaspoon crushed red pepper

1/2 teaspoon dried oregano

1 tablespoon top-quality extra-virgin olive oil

Primo Pizza Dough for the Grill (page 36)

1. Fire up the grill for a two-level fire capable of cooking at the same time on both high heat (1 to 2 seconds with the hand test) and medium-low heat (5 to 6 seconds with the hand test); see page 6.

2. Toss together the salad topping ingredients in a medium-size bowl; cover and refrigerate until needed. Combine the cheese topping ingredients in a medium-size bowl.

3. Place the toppings, oil, and an oil brush within easy reach of the grill. The process must go quickly once you begin cooking. Place a baking sheet on a convenient work surface near the grill and have a large spatula or pizza peel handy.

4. Place the first crust on the grill, laying it directly on the cooking grate over high heat. Grill, uncovered, for 1 to 1 1/2 minutes, until the crust becomes firm but is still flexible. Don't worry about any bubbles that form on the crust as they will be flattened when you turn over the crust in the next step.

5. Using the spatula or peel, flip the crust onto the baking sheet, cooked side up. Immediately brush with half of the oil and sprinkle with half of the cheese mixture. Quickly return the pizza to the grill (without the baking sheet), uncooked side down. Arrange the pie so that half of it is over high heat and the other half is over medium-low. Cook the pizza for another 3 to 4 minutes, rotating it in quarter turns every 30 to 45 seconds. This may sound awkward but becomes second nature very quickly. Using the spatula to lift the edge slightly, check the bottom during the last minute or two, rotating a bit faster or slower if needed to get a uniformly brown, crisp crust. Near the end of the cooking, with about 1 minute left, top the pizza with half of the salad topping.

6. Slice the pizza into wedges and serve immediately. Repeat the process for your second pizza.

PIZZA POINTERS FOR THE GRILL

Unless you're ready to invest serious money in a dedicated pizza oven, a grill offers the closest results to authentic pizza at home. Our recipe instructions call for rotating the pizza, after its initial quick toasting on high heat, between the hot and medium-low areas of a two-level fire. It's easier than it may sound, and from our experience, it makes an important difference in the results. We've tried a variety of approaches, but nothing else has worked as well as alternating between periods of high-heat crisping and low-heat finishing. Some large and powerful grills provide means other than rotation to accomplish the goal, but none of them is any more simple or sure than turning the pizza as you cook.

The hands-on nature of the process requires an open grill. Some people do bake pizzas in a covered grill, usually over medium heat, but the outcome is considerably different and, we think, not nearly as good.

Because of the attention needed with the rotation method, we always grill one pizza at a time, serving each as it's ready and continuing to cook until the last one is done. Be sure to have all the ingredients ready and handy when you start to work. The grilling goes so quickly you won't have time to run back to the kitchen for anything missing. Unless a recipe specifically calls for cold toppings, as in our Hot and Cool Pizza (page 40), the ingredients should be warm or at room temperature before you begin. With all the necessities in place, apply your showman's touch, adding a bit of this and a bunch of that with Neapolitan flair.

PECORINO PIZZA WITH ARTICHOKES

This was an easy choice for our top 100 grill dishes, picked by both of us on our original list of nominations. The light, pleasant saltiness of pecorino, an aged cheese made from sheep's milk, complements the mild sweetness of sautéed artichokes and leeks on this pizza. Frozen (but not canned) artichoke hearts work fine in this case, saving the extra preparation effort needed for the fresh ingredient. **MAKES TWO 11-INCH PIZZAS**

VEGETABLE TOPPING

3 tablespoons top-quality extra-virgin olive oil

2 cups chopped leeks

One 9-ounce package frozen artichoke hearts, thawed, blotted of moisture, and sliced thin (about 2 cups)

Juice of $1/2$ lemon

$1/2$ teaspoon kosher salt or coarse sea salt, or more to taste

CHEESE TOPPING

$3/4$ cup grated mozzarella or fontina, at room temperature

$1/2$ cup grated pecorino, preferably Pecorino Romano, at room temperature

1 garlic clove, minced

$1/2$ to 1 teaspoon crushed red pepper

$1/2$ teaspoon crumbled dried oregano

$1/2$ teaspoon crumbled dried thyme

1 tablespoon top-quality extra-virgin olive oil

$1/4$ cup slivered, drained oil-packed sun-dried tomatoes or 1 medium-size red bell pepper, roasted (see Grilling Tip on page 45), peeled, and sliced into thin strips

1/4 cup pine nuts (optional)

Primo Pizza Dough for the Grill (page 36)

1. To prepare the vegetable topping, first warm the oil in a heavy nonreactive skillet over medium heat. Sauté the leeks for several minutes until limp. Add the artichoke hearts and cook for another few minutes, until both the leeks and artichokes are tender. Stir in the lemon juice and salt; remove from the heat and set aside.

2. Fire up the grill for a two-level fire capable of cooking at the same time on both high heat (1 to 2 seconds with the hand test) and medium-low heat (5 to 6 seconds with the hand test); see page 6.

3. Combine the cheese topping ingredients in a medium-size bowl.

4. Place the vegetable and cheese mixtures, oil, tomatoes, pine nuts (if using), and an oil brush within easy reach of the grill. The process must go quickly once you begin cooking. Place a baking sheet on a convenient work surface near the grill and have a large spatula or pizza peel handy.

5. Place the first crust on the grill, laying it directly on the cooking grate over high heat. Grill, uncovered, for 1 to 1 1/2 minutes, until the crust becomes firm but is still flexible. Don't worry about any bubbles that form on the crust as they will be flattened when you turn over the crust in the next step.

6. Using the spatula or peel, flip the crust onto the baking sheet, cooked side up. Immediately brush with half of the oil, sprinkle with half of the cheese mixture, and top with half of the vegetable topping, tomatoes, and pine nuts, if using. Quickly return the pizza to the grill (without the baking sheet), uncooked side down. Arrange the pie so that half of it is over high heat and the other half is over medium-low. Cook the pizza for another 3 to 4 minutes, rotating it in quarter turns every 30 to 45 seconds. This may sound awkward but becomes second nature very quickly. Using the spatula to lift the edge slightly, check the bottom during the last minute or two, rotating a bit faster or slower if needed to get a uniformly brown, crisp crust.

7. Slice the pizza into wedges and serve immediately. Repeat the process for your second pizza.

To roast a single pepper, the easiest method is to set it on the burner of a gas stove or gas grill turned on high, or over a hot charcoal fire. Let the skin blacken and blister on all sides, turning it as needed. When uniformly blackened, place in a plastic or paper bag, close, and let it steam until cool enough to handle. Pull the charred loose skin from the pepper. Then seed and stem before using.

pecorino, an aged cheese made from sheep's milk, complements the mild sweetness of sautéed artichokes and leeks

WHITE PIZZA

White pizza (or *pizza bianca*) leaves off the standard tomato sauce. In this twist, we substitute silky crème fraîche. Don't be tempted to use sour cream in its place, as it can break down when exposed to the high heat of the grill. This style of pizza is really good served with a cruet of spicy olive oil to pass. Should you wish to add a little meat, we suggest thin-sliced Canadian bacon or ham, or crisp bacon crumbles. **MAKES TWO 11-INCH PIZZAS**

> 3/4 cup crème fraîche, at room temperature
>
> 1/4 cup freshly grated Parmigiano-Reggiano, at room temperature
>
> 2 teaspoons top-quality extra-virgin olive oil
>
> 1/3 cup slivered strong-flavored brine- or oil-cured black olives
>
> Primo Pizza Dough for the Grill (page 36)

1. Fire up the grill for a two-level fire capable of cooking at the same time on both high heat (1 to 2 seconds with the hand test) and medium-low heat (5 to 6 seconds with the hand test); see page 6.

2. Stir together the crème fraîche and Parmigiano-Reggiano. Place the crème fraîche mixture, oil, olives, and an oil brush within easy reach of the grill. The process must go quickly once you begin cooking. Place a baking sheet on a convenient work surface near the grill and have a large spatula or pizza peel handy.

3. Place the first crust on the grill, laying it directly on the cooking grate over high heat. Grill, uncovered, for 1 to 1 1/2 minutes, until the crust becomes firm but is still flexible. Don't worry about any bubbles that form on the crust as they will be flattened when you turn over the crust in the next step.

4. Using the spatula or peel, flip the crust onto the baking sheet, cooked side up. Immediately spoon on half of the oil, smearing it around. Then spoon on half of the crème fraîche mixture and top with half of the olives. Quickly return the pizza to the grill (without the baking sheet), uncooked side down. Arrange the pie so that half of it is over high heat and the other half is over medium-low. Cook the pizza for another

3 to 5 minutes, rotating it in quarter turns every 30 to 45 seconds. This may sound awkward but becomes second nature very quickly. Using the spatula to lift the edge slightly, check the bottom during the last minute or two, rotating a bit faster or slower if needed to get a uniformly brown, crisp crust.

5. Slice the pizza into wedges and serve immediately. Repeat the process for your second pizza.

> pizza bianca *leaves off the standard tomato sauce, and we substitute silky crème fraîche*

FIRED ONION FLATBREAD

We use pizza dough for this flatbread but leave off both tomatoes and cheese, relying instead on caramelized onions for the primary flavor. **MAKES TWO 11-INCH FLATBREADS**

ONION TOPPING

6 tablespoons top-quality extra-virgin olive oil

2 medium-size onions, thinly sliced

2 tablespoons minced fresh marjoram or 1 teaspoon crumbled dried marjoram

1 teaspoon sugar

1 teaspoon kosher salt or coarse sea salt, or more to taste

1 to 2 tablespoons top-quality extra-virgin olive oil

Coarsely ground black pepper

1/3 cup slivered green olives (optional)

Primo Pizza Dough for the Grill (page 36)

1. To prepare the onion topping, first warm the oil in a large, heavy skillet over medium-low heat. Stir in the onions, sprinkle them with the marjoram, sugar, and salt, and cook, covered, for 6 to 8 minutes, until they begin to turn golden, shaking them occasionally. Remove the cover and continue to cook, stirring occasionally, until the liquid evaporates and the onions are medium brown and chewy, another 10 to 15 minutes. (The topping can be prepared a day ahead and stored, covered, in the refrigerator. Rewarm before proceeding.)

2. Fire up the grill for a two-level fire capable of cooking at the same time on both high heat (1 to 2 seconds with the hand test) and medium-low heat (5 to 6 seconds with the hand test); see page 6.

3. Place the onion topping, pepper, oil, olives (if using), and an oil brush within easy reach of the grill. The process must go quickly once you begin cooking. Place a baking

sheet on a convenient work surface near the grill and have a large spatula or pizza peel handy.

4. Place the first crust on the grill, laying it directly on the cooking grate over high heat. Grill, uncovered, for 1 to 1¹/2 minutes, until the crust becomes firm but is still flexible. Don't worry about any bubbles that form on the crust as they will be flattened when you turn over the crust in the next step.

5. Using the spatula or peel, flip the crust onto the baking sheet, cooked side up. Immediately brush with half of the oil and top with half of the onions, a good sprinkling of pepper, and half of the olives, if using. Quickly return the bread to the grill (without the baking sheet), uncooked side down. Arrange the crust so that half of it is over high heat and the other half is over medium-low. Cook the bread for another 3 to 5 minutes, rotating it in quarter turns every 30 to 45 seconds. This may sound awkward but becomes second nature very quickly. Using the spatula to lift the edge slightly, check the bottom during the last minute, rotating a bit faster or slower if needed to get a uniformly brown, crisp crust.

6. Slice or tear the bread into wedges and serve immediately. Repeat the process for your second flatbread.

BLUE CORN AND GREEN CHILE PIZZA

New Mexicans put green chile in or on all kinds of food, including pizza. We take the cross-cultural blending of Italian and southwestern even further here, adding New Mexico's distinctive blue cornmeal to the dough and making a pesto topping with cilantro instead of basil. **MAKES TWO 10-INCH PIZZAS**

NEW MEXICO PIZZA DOUGH

$1^1/_2$ cups bread flour (or more if needed)

$1/_2$ cup stone-ground blue cornmeal or other cornmeal

1 teaspoon salt

1 envelope rapid-rise yeast (about $2^1/_2$ teaspoons)

$3/_4$ cup lukewarm water, 105° to 115°F

1 tablespoon extra-virgin olive oil

1 garlic clove, minced

CILANTRO PESTO

1 cup lightly packed chopped fresh cilantro

2 tablespoons *pepitas* (hulled pumpkin seeds) or slivered almonds

1 garlic clove, peeled

$1/_4$ cup grated dry (aged) Jack, Cotija, Pecorino Romano, or Parmigiano-Reggiano

6 tablespoons extra-virgin olive oil

Kosher salt or coarse sea salt

Freshly ground black pepper

$1^1/_4$ cups grated asadero, Monterey Jack, or pepper Jack cheese, at room temperature

1 cup shredded grilled or smoked chicken breast (optional)

2 small red-ripe plum tomatoes, chopped

1/2 to 3/4 cup chopped fresh or (thawed) frozen mild green chiles, such as New Mexican or Anaheim, at room temperature

Crushed red pepper

1. Prepare the pizza crust. In a food processor, pulse together the flour, cornmeal, salt, and yeast. With the motor running, add the water, all but 1/2 teaspoon of the oil, and the garlic. Continue processing for about 30 seconds more, until the dough forms a fairly cohesive ball that is smooth and elastic. If it remains sticky, add another tablespoon or two of flour.

2. Knead the dough a few times on a floured work surface, forming it into a ball. Pour the remaining 1/2 teaspoon oil into a large bowl and add the dough, turning it around and over until coated with oil. Cover with a damp cloth. Set the dough in a warm, draft-free spot and let it rise until doubled in volume, about 1 hour.

3. Punch the dough down on a floured surface and let it rest for 10 minutes. Roll the dough into two thin disks, about 10 inches in diameter, stretching and prodding it with your fingers, too. (The dough is ready to use at this point, or can be saved for later in the refrigerator or freezer. Line a baking sheet with wax paper and stack the crusts on it, with another sheet of wax paper between the crusts. Chill the crusts on the baking sheet for about 30 minutes to firm the dough, then remove from the baking sheet and wrap the crusts in plastic wrap before storing. The dough can be refrigerated for up to 3 days or frozen for 1 month. Bring the crusts back to room temperature before proceeding.)

4. Fire up the grill for a two-level fire capable of cooking at the same time on both high heat (1 to 2 seconds with the hand test) and medium-low heat (5 to 6 seconds with the hand test); see page 6.

5. To prepare the cilantro pesto, combine the cilantro, *pepitas*, garlic, and cheese in a food processor and pulse to blend. With the motor still running, add the oil in a thin, steady drizzle. Add salt and pepper to taste, and combine again.

6. Place the pesto, a spoon for the pesto, and the remaining ingredients within easy reach of the grill. The process must go quickly once you begin cooking. Place a baking sheet on a convenient work surface near the grill and have a large spatula or pizza peel handy.

7. Place the first crust on the grill, laying it directly on the cooking grate over high heat. Grill, uncovered, for 1 to 1½ minutes, until the crust becomes firm but is still flexible. Don't worry about any bubbles that form on the crust as they will be flattened when you turn over the crust in the next step.

8. Using the spatula or peel, flip the crust onto the baking sheet, cooked side up. Immediately brush with half each of the pesto, cheese, chicken (if using), tomatoes, and green chile, and top with a sprinkling of red pepper. Quickly return the pizza to the grill (without the baking sheet), uncooked side down. Arrange the pie so that half of it is over high heat and the other half is over medium-low. Cook the pizza for another 3 to 4 minutes, rotating it in quarter turns every 30 to 45 seconds. This may sound awkward but becomes second nature very quickly. Using the spatula to lift the edge slightly, check the bottom during the last minute or two, rotating a bit faster or slower if needed to get a uniformly brown, crisp crust.

9. Slice the pizza into wedges and serve immediately. Repeat the process for your second pizza.

takes the cross-cultural blending of Italian and southwestern even further

WHY MEN MAN THE GRILL

Esquire magazine's 1949 *Handbook for Hosts* (Grosset & Dunlap) claims that every adult male is attracted to grilling because he retains "some of the qualities of a small boy. He is secretly plagued by a spirit of pyromania and he delights in playing with fires." Wives encourage the impulse, the editors maintain, because they are sick of cooking and would never be expected to do any outdoors. "A woman presiding over a barbecue grill looks as incongruous as a man engaged in doing a trifle of lacy tatting." Bachelors have even more reason than husbands to pursue the craft, according to the theory, because it attracts the opposite sex. *Esquire* supported this claim with a story about a single man grilling a steak for breakfast and arousing the interest of his sunbathing neighbor, "a most delectable young lady, unchastely clad in the briefest possible sun suit."

BLAZING BURGERS AND HAUTE DOGS

ALL-AMERICAN
BACKYARD BURGERS

Despite an abundance of speculation, nobody knows for sure who first put the German-inspired Hamburg steak on a bun. The rest of the story is far clearer. The sandwich became an instant hit at roadside cafés on the earliest American highways, and then surged again in popularity when the outdoor grilling revolution began right after World War II. Grilling wasn't really a big advance over frying as a cooking method for the meat, but the open-air setting and the fun of handheld food quickly made the backyard burger into a hallmark American meal. **SERVES 4**

> 2/3 cup mayonnaise
>
> 2 tablespoons ketchup
>
> 1 1/2 to 2 pounds freshly ground beef chuck or brisket (see Grilling Tip on page 60)
>
> 1 teaspoon kosher salt or coarse sea salt
>
> 3/4 teaspoon freshly ground black pepper
>
> 4 large hamburger buns
>
> 8 thin slices cheddar, Monterey Jack, Colby, or American cheese, at room temperature (optional)
>
> 4 large, thick slices red-ripe tomato
>
> 4 thin slices red onion
>
> Dill pickle slices (optional)
>
> Crisp iceberg lettuce leaves

1. Fire up the grill for a two-level fire capable of cooking at the same time on both high heat (1 to 2 seconds with the hand test) and medium heat (4 to 5 seconds with the hand test); see page 6.

2. Combine the mayonnaise and ketchup in a small bowl; cover and refrigerate until serving time.

3. Mix together the ground beef, salt, and pepper. Gently form the mixture into 4 patties, each 1/2 to 3/4 inch thick. The patties should hold together firmly, but don't compact them or handle them any longer than necessary.

4. Grill the burgers, uncovered, over high heat for 1 1/2 minutes per side. Move the burgers over to medium heat and rotate a half turn for crisscross grill marks. Don't, under any circumstances, press down on the burgers with the spatula. Cook for 3 1/2 to 4 minutes per side for medium doneness, until crusty and richly brown with a slight hint of pink at the center. Toast the buns at the edge of the grill if you wish. If you plan to make cheeseburgers, place two overlapping slices on each burger a few minutes before you remove them from the grill.

5. Spoon the mayonnaise-ketchup mixture generously over both sides of a bun. Add a burger, slice of tomato and onion, pickles if you wish, and lettuce, and repeat with the remaining burgers and ingredients. Eat the burgers hot, squeezing firmly to release and combine the juices.

HEALTHY GROUND BEEF

A nineteenth-century American physician, Dr. James Henry Salisbury, left us the enduring legacy of the Salisbury steak, a staple for generations in our country. He recommended everyone eat ground beef three times a day to prevent and treat colitis, anemia, asthma, rheumatism, tuberculosis, and other ills. Salisbury even thought the diet would relieve hardening of the arteries, a notion we love to mention to doctors.

BERGHOFF'S CHICAGO BEER BURGERS

When you want to fuss a bit with burgers, here's one of our favorite techniques, created by caterer-restaurateur Carlyn Berghoff and her former chef David Norman. With it, the imaginative cooks offer a toast to a Chicago institution, The Berghoff, founded by Carlyn's great-grandfather in 1898. Still in the family, the quintessential Loop restaurant remains true to its roots, serving robust food with local beer. Thanks to Carlyn and Dave, as well as to Marcel Desaulniers for allowing us to borrow the recipe, featured originally in his wonderful book *The Burger Meisters* (Simon & Schuster, 1993). **SERVES 4**

MUSHROOM-BEER KETCHUP

1 tablespoon unsalted butter

1 small onion, chopped

4 ounces button mushrooms, stems trimmed and sliced

6 tablespoons medium-bodied beer

1/3 cup ketchup

1 tablespoon distilled white vinegar

1/4 teaspoon sugar

1/4 teaspoon kosher salt or coarse sea salt

BEER-BRAISED ONIONS

1 tablespoon unsalted butter

1 large onion, sliced thin

1 cup medium-bodied beer

1 teaspoon sugar

1/2 teaspoon kosher salt or coarse sea salt

1 1/2 pounds freshly ground beef chuck

2 tablespoons medium-bodied beer

1/2 teaspoon Tabasco or other hot pepper sauce

1/4 teaspoon Worcestershire sauce

Kosher salt or coarse sea salt

Freshly ground black pepper

Four 1/2-ounce slices brick cheese or other pungent cheese such as sharp or extra-sharp cheddar, at room temperature

4 hamburger buns, preferably bakery-made

1. At least 24 hours before you plan to grill the burgers, prepare the ketchup. Melt the butter in a large, heavy saucepan over medium heat. Add the onion and mushrooms and sauté until just tender, 3 to 4 minutes. Remove the saucepan from the heat and add the beer, ketchup, vinegar, sugar, and salt. Use a hand-held immersion blender to puree the mixture, or spoon it into a blender or food processor and puree. Return the ketchup to the saucepan (if needed), return the heat to medium, and bring the mixture to a boil. Reduce the ketchup until slightly thickened, about 12 minutes. Remove from the heat and set aside to cool. Spoon the ketchup into a nonreactive container and refrigerate for at least 1 day or up to 3 days.

2. To prepare the onions, melt the butter in a large, heavy saucepan over medium-high heat. Add the onion and sauté, stirring frequently, until very tender, 5 to 6 minutes. Add 3/4 cup of the beer, the sugar, and salt. Cook, stirring occasionally, until all of the beer has been absorbed by the onions and they begin to brown lightly, 16 to 18 minutes. Add the remaining 1/4 cup beer and bring to a simmer. Keep the onions warm.

3. Fire up the grill for a two-level fire capable of cooking at the same time on both high heat (1 to 2 seconds with the hand test) and medium heat (4 to 5 seconds with the hand test); see page 6.

4. In a large bowl, gently but thoroughly combine the ground chuck, beer, Tabasco, Worcestershire, and salt and pepper to taste. Gently form the mixture into 4 patties, each 1/2 to 3/4 inch thick. The patties should hold together firmly, but don't compact them or handle them any longer than necessary.

5. Grill the burgers, uncovered, over high heat for 1 1/2 minutes per side. Move the burgers over to medium heat and rotate a half turn for crisscross grill marks. Don't, under any circumstances, press down on the burgers with the spatula. Cook for 3 1/2 to 4

minutes per side for medium doneness, until crusty and richly brown with a slight hint of pink at the center. Top with the cheese in the last few minutes of cooking. Toast the buns at the edge of the grill.

6. Serve the burgers hot on the toasted buns, topped with some of the braised onions, with the ketchup on the side.

GRILLING TIP

Using freshly ground beef always enhances the flavor of a burger. Many butchers, even in chain supermarkets, will grind chuck or brisket for you on request, but you should be prepared to cook it that day to retain the taste advantage. The best approach is to grind the meat yourself at home right before you grill. Use a meat grinder or grinding attachment on a mixer, if you have either, or you can use a food processor. Take the beef directly from the refrigerator and cut it into chunks or strips. In an average-size processor, grind the meat one burger at a time, pulsing it with the regular chopping blade. For superior taste and texture, we like a grind slightly coarser than the regular supermarket style. After you go to this much effort, it's best to grill your burgers to medium doneness. The prized juiciness is lost with well-done meat.

CARIBBEAN CURRY BURGERS

Chef Ruedi Portmann created this burger, inspired by Caribbean curries, at the Curtain Bluff resort on Antigua. Here's his simple yet masterful recipe, as sassy as a calypso. **SERVES 4**

CARIBBEAN CURRY SAUCE

1/2 cup mayonnaise

1/2 cup sour cream

1/4 cup mango chutney, any large chunks of fruit finely chopped

2 to 3 teaspoons curry powder

1 1/2 pounds freshly ground beef chuck

1 1/2 teaspoons freshly ground black pepper

1 teaspoon kosher salt or coarse sea salt

4 kaiser rolls or other large rolls

4 slices red onion

Iceberg or butter lettuce leaves

Caribbean scotch bonnet or habanero hot sauce (optional)

1. Mix together the curry sauce ingredients in a medium-size bowl, adding as much of the curry powder as appeals to you. (The sauce can be prepared several days ahead and refrigerated.)

2. Fire up the grill for a two-level fire capable of cooking at the same time on both high heat (1 to 2 seconds with the hand test) and medium heat (4 to 5 seconds with the hand test); see page 6.

3. In a large bowl, combine the ground chuck, pepper, and salt. Gently form the mixture into 4 patties, each 1/2 to 3/4 inch thick. The patties should hold together firmly, but don't compact them or handle them any longer than necessary.

4. Grill the burgers, uncovered, over high heat for 1 1/2 minutes per side. Move the burgers over to medium heat and rotate a half turn for crisscross grill marks. Don't, under

any circumstances, press down on the burgers with the spatula. Cook for 3^1/$_2$ to 4 minutes per side for medium doneness, until crusty and richly brown with a slight hint of pink at the center. Toast the buns at the edge of the grill if you wish.

5. Serve the burgers hot on the buns with an onion slice, lettuce, generous spoonfuls of curry sauce, and, if you wish, a little splash of Caribbean hot sauce. (Use any leftover curry sauce to enhance dishes such as a chicken or shrimp salad.)

GREAT PLAINS BISON BURGERS

The American bison, popularly known as the buffalo, makes a fine burger. It tastes much like grass-fed beef, but with a bit more minerality. The meat is leaner, however, so to avoid overcooking, be sure to time and watch it carefully on the grill. **SERVES 4**

DRY RUB

2 tablespoons smoked salt or hickory salt

1 tablespoon coarsely ground black pepper

4 slices red onion, about 1/3 inch thick

Vegetable oil spray

1 1/2 pounds ground bison

4 large hamburger buns

Mayonnaise

Butter lettuce leaves

1. Fire up the grill for a two-level fire capable of cooking at the same time on both high heat (1 to 2 seconds with the hand test) and medium heat (4 to 5 seconds with the hand test); see page 6.

2. Combine the salt and pepper for the dry rub. Mix 1 teaspoon of the dry rub into the bison meat. Gently form the mixture into 4 patties, each 1/2 to 3/4 inch thick. The patties should hold together firmly, but don't compact them or handle them any longer than necessary. Pat the patties with the remaining dry rub.

3. Spray the onions slices on both sides with oil. Arrange the onions over medium heat and cook, uncovered, until tender, 12 to 15 minutes total, turning three times and rotating a half turn for crisscross grill marks. If you have enough grate space, you can begin cooking the burgers while the onions finish.

4. Grill the burgers, uncovered, over high heat for 1 minute per side. Move the burgers over to medium heat and rotate a half turn for crisscross grill marks. Don't, under

any circumstances, press down on the burgers with the spatula. Cook for 2 1/2 to 3 minutes per side for medium doneness, until richly brown with a pink center. Toast the buns at the edge of the grill if you wish.

5. Spoon mayonnaise generously on both sides of the buns. Arrange a burger on each bun, then top with a grilled onion slice and a couple of lettuce leaves. Serve immediately.

the American bison, popularly known as the buffalo, makes a fine burger

ROSEMARY AND MINT LAMB BURGERS

In a blind tasting, many burger fans would find that they like lamb burgers better than hamburgers. The meat is earthier, somehow more soulful, than beef, particularly when it's fresh, pasture-grazed lamb that hasn't been shipped frozen from halfway around the world. All grillers should have a version in their repertoire. **SERVES 4**

1¹/₂ pounds freshly ground lamb, preferably shoulder

¹/₂ cup minced fresh mint

2 tablespoons finely minced fresh rosemary or 1¹/₂ tablespoons lightly packed finely crumbled dried rosemary

1 teaspoon kosher salt or coarse sea salt

8 slices sourdough bread

Mayonnaise

1. Fire up the grill, bringing the temperature to medium (4 to 5 seconds with the hand test).

2. In a medium-size bowl, mix together the ground lamb, mint, rosemary, and salt. Gently form the mixture into 4 patties, each ¹/₂ to ³/₄ inch thick. The patties should hold together firmly, but don't compact them or handle them any longer than necessary.

3. Grill, uncovered, for a total of 5 to 5¹/₂ minutes for medium-rare. Rotate a half turn, halfway through cooking on each side, for crisscross grill marks. Toast the bread at the edge of the grill if you wish.

4. Serve each burger between two slices of sourdough, slathered with mayonnaise.

HERB-RUBBED TURKEY BURGERS

We eat these primarily because they taste great, not because of the presumed health benefits. As with beef and lamb, it's best for the turkey to be freshly ground, by you or the butcher at your market. Use thigh meat for maximum flavor, mixed with a little Worcestershire sauce and mustard, then covered with a dry spice rub. If turkey thighs are unavailable, choose chicken thighs over turkey breast meat. Like lamb burgers, turkey patties grill best over a steady medium flame, but unlike other burgers, they should be cooked almost well done.
SERVES 4

1/2 cup mayonnaise

2 to 3 tablespoons Dijon mustard

DRY RUB

1 tablespoon plus 1 teaspoon crumbled dried thyme

2 teaspoons crumbled dried sage

2 teaspoons freshly ground black pepper

1 1/2 teaspoons kosher salt or coarse sea salt

1 teaspoon ground white pepper

1 1/2 pounds freshly ground turkey thighs

1 1/2 teaspoons Dijon mustard

1 1/2 teaspoons Worcestershire sauce

4 onion rolls or large hamburger buns

Butter lettuce leaves or shredded red cabbage

1. Fire up the grill, bringing the temperature to medium (4 to 5 seconds with the hand test).

2. Combine the mayonnaise and mustard in a small bowl and reserve.

3. Mix together the dry rub ingredients and set aside. Combine the ground turkey, mustard, and Worcestershire in a large bowl. Gently form the mixture into 4 patties, each about 1/2 inch thick. The patties should hold together firmly, but don't compact them or handle them any longer than necessary. If the meat becomes too soft to form, put it in the refrigerator or freezer briefly. Sprinkle the dry rub evenly over both sides of each burger.

4. Grill the burgers, uncovered, for 8 to 9 minutes per side, until medium-brown and crisp with a fully cooked interior, 165°F on an instant-read thermometer inserted into a burger from its side. Rotate a half turn, halfway through cooking on each side, for crisscross grill marks. Toast the rolls at the edge of the grill if you wish.

5. Spread the mayonnaise-mustard mixture on both halves of each roll, then add the burgers and top with lettuce. Serve immediately.

GRILLING TIP

If turkey makes you think of Thanksgiving, go with the notion, replacing the

mayo-mustard with cranberry chutney or cranberry sauce.

PORTOBELLO BURGERS

Nothing makes a finer a vegetarian "burger" than a portobello mushroom cap. Though we are hardly vegetarians ourselves, this was a clear choice to be among our 100 favorite dishes. To enhance the flavor we bathe the portobellos prior to cooking in equal parts olive oil, vinegar, and soy. **SERVES 4**

MARINADE

1/4 cup extra-virgin olive oil

1/4 cup inexpensive balsamic vinegar

1/4 cup soy sauce

3 garlic cloves, minced

4 portobello mushroom caps (stems reserved for another purpose), each about 5 inches in diameter

RED BELL PEPPER MAYONNAISE

1/2 medium-size red bell pepper

1/3 cup mayonnaise

1 teaspoon extra-virgin olive oil

Pinch of cayenne pepper

4 thin slices mozzarella or fontina cheese, each large enough to cover a mushroom cap (optional)

4 kaiser rolls or other large, crusty rolls

Butter lettuce leaves

4 slices red-ripe tomato

1. At least 30 minutes and up to 2 hours before you plan to grill, combine the marinade ingredients in a medium-size bowl. Place the mushrooms in a large zipper-top plastic bag, pour the marinade over them, and let sit at room temperature. Turn the bag occasionally if needed to saturate the surfaces with the marinade.

2. To make the mayonnaise, spear the red pepper with a fork and hold it, skin side down, directly over a stove burner briefly until the skin blackens and blisters. Transfer the pepper to a plastic or paper bag, close, and let it steam until cool enough to handle. Pull the loose skin from the pepper. Cut the pepper into several chunks and puree with the other mayonnaise ingredients in a small food processor or blender. Refrigerate until serving time.

3. Fire up the grill, bringing the temperature to medium (4 to 5 seconds with the hand test).

4. Drain the mushroom caps, discarding the marinade. Transfer the mushrooms to the cooking grate, cap sides up, so you immediately caramelize some of the accumulated juice on their undersides. Grill, uncovered, for 8 to 10 minutes, turning the mushrooms twice and topping each with a cheese slice, if you wish, when the mushrooms are again cap sides up. Toast the rolls on the edge of the grill if you wish.

5. Place the mushrooms on the toasted rolls and add lettuce, tomato slices, and dollops of the mayonnaise. Serve hot.

MARK TWAIN ON HEALTHY LIVING

"I doubt if God has given us any refreshment which, taken in moderation, is unwholesome, except microbes. Yet there are people who strictly deprive themselves of each and every eatable, drinkable and smokeable which has in any way acquired a shady reputation. They pay this price for health. And health is all they get for it. How strange it is! It is like paying out your whole fortune for a cow that has gone dry."

—MARK TWAIN, *THE AUTOBIOGRAPHY OF MARK TWAIN* (CHARLES NEIDER, EDITOR) (1961)

PACIFIC RIM TUNA BURGERS

Tuna steaks make super burgers, more uptown than their peers and every bit as tasty. Because you're working with fairly thin steaks, chill them until they're good and cold before putting them on the grill, to make sure they don't get too cooked in the center before the surface is nicely colored. **SERVES 4**

WASABI-SCALLION MAYONNAISE

1/2 cup mayonnaise

2 scallions, roots and limp tops trimmed, minced

1 teaspoon wasabi paste, or more to taste

1 tablespoon teriyaki sauce

2 teaspoons Asian toasted sesame oil

Two 1-inch-thick tuna steaks (about 12 ounces each), cut horizontally in half to create four 1/2-inch-thick steaks, chilled

Kosher salt or coarse sea salt

8 slices good-quality white bread

Trimmed watercress, butter lettuce leaves, or shredded romaine

1. Stir together the mayonnaise ingredients in a small bowl and reserve.

2. Fire up the grill, bringing the temperature to medium-high (3 seconds with the hand test). Oil the cooking grate.

3. Stir together the teriyaki sauce and oil, and coat the steaks very lightly with the mixture. Sprinkle lightly with salt.

4. Grill the steaks, uncovered, for 2 to 3 minutes per side, until lightly browned with a touch of pink at the very center. Toast the bread at the edge of the grill if you wish.

5. Spread mayonnaise on each of the bread slices. Top half with the tuna steaks and watercress. Crown with remaining bread slices. Serve hot.

DOGGONE GOOD HOT DOG

An increasing number of meat markets are making specialty dogs of their own, usually handcrafted creations that emulate the original American frankfurters. If you find any of these, try them for sure, but supermarkets also sell much better dogs than they did in the recent past, including brands such as Hebrew National, Nathan's, Niman Ranch, Vienna Beef, and Oscar Mayer Original.

SERVES A PARTY

> 1 or 2 hot dogs per person
>
> Hot dog buns
>
> Sweet pickle relish, preferably made with mustard
>
> Chopped onions (optional)
>
> Creole, brown, yellow, or other favorite mustard

1. Fire up the grill, bringing the temperature to high (1 to 2 seconds with the hand test).

2. Grill the wieners, uncovered, for 3 to 5 minutes, or until deeply browned, rolling to crisp them all the way around. Toast the buns on the edge of the grill if you wish.

3. Arrange the dogs on the buns and top with hearty spoonfuls of relish and, if you wish, onions. Add squiggles of mustard to finish them off and serve immediately. Plates aren't necessary, but napkins are.

GRILLING TIP

When you grill a precooked sausage like a hot dog, the goal is to crust the skin and create a bold, contrasting texture between the seared surface and the juicy interior. You don't need to worry about doneness or exact timing, but you do want to roll the doggie around for a thorough crisping that stops well short of the incineration once popular at wiener roasts.

BRATWURST ROLL, SHEBOYGAN-STYLE

Uncooked bratwursts, like any other uncooked sausage, can simply go on the grill over medium heat for long enough to be cooked through. However, these beer-soaked brats take their cue from the noteworthy style of Sheboygan, Wisconsin. Folks in the German-settled bastion of brats and brew sear the sausages over fire, then turn them into hearty sandwiches, sometimes with multiple toppings. **SERVES 4**

BREW MARINADE

12 ounces (1 1/2 cups) beer

1/2 large onion, chopped

3 tablespoons brown mustard

1/2 teaspoon caraway seeds

8 uncooked bratwursts (4 to 5 ounces each; see Grilling Tip on page 73), split lengthwise

CARAWAY KRAUT

2 tablespoons butter

1 small onion, chopped

2 teaspoons caraway seeds

2 teaspoons brown mustard

2 cups drained sauerkraut

4 kaiser rolls or other large rolls or 4 large slices rye or sourdough bread, each cut in half

Brown mustard

4 thin slices Swiss, provolone, Gouda, or Gruyère cheese (optional)

Chopped dill pickles (optional)

1. Bring the marinade ingredients to a boil in a large saucepan. Simmer for 5 minutes. Add the halved bratwursts to the marinade, reduce the heat to low, cover, and cook for 15 minutes. Remove the saucepan from the heat but leave the brats in the liquid to steep while you heat the grill.

2. Fire up the grill, bringing the temperature to high (1 to 2 seconds with the hand test).

3. To prepare the kraut, melt the butter in a medium-size saucepan over medium heat. Stir in the onion and caraway and cook for 1 to 2 minutes, just until the onion turns translucent. Add the mustard and sauerkraut and heat through. Keep warm.

4. Drain the brats, discarding the marinade. Grill the brats, uncovered, for about 2 minutes per side, until well browned and crusty but still juicy. Toast the rolls on the edge of the grill if you wish.

5. Assemble the sandwiches, slathering each toasted roll with mustard. Arrange 2 brats on each roll, then add a slice of cheese (if using), followed by a generous spoonful of the kraut. Sprinkle with chopped dill pickle, if you wish. Serve immediately, squeezing to mingle the juices and ingredients.

GRILLING TIP

In recipes that call for uncooked sausage, you can usually substitute the same kind of precooked sausage when available, eliminating the need for a two-level fire and cutting the total grilling time in half. This bratwurst is an exception. Here it's important to start with uncooked sausage because of the advance simmering and steeping in beer. Precooked sausage won't absorb the marinade fully and will dry out during the pot-to-grill cooking process.

ITALIAN SAUSAGE SANDWICH

Dogs, brats, and many other sausages are scrumptious topped with sauerkraut, but a fresh slaw topping can add a brighter, crisper note to these preparations. Fennel and mild peppers pair especially well with Italian sausage. **SERVES 4**

FENNEL SLAW

1 medium-size fennel bulb, trimmed, bulb sliced thin, then cut into thin matchsticks

1 small red or yellow bell pepper, seeded and cut into thin matchsticks

1 carrot, peeled and shredded

1/2 small red onion, sliced into thin half-moons

3 tablespoons extra-virgin olive oil

1 tablespoon red wine vinegar

1 small garlic clove, minced

1/2 teaspoon kosher salt or coarse sea salt

4 uncooked sweet or hot Italian sausages (5 to 6 ounces each)

4 Italian or hoagie rolls

4 thin slices provolone cheese, at room temperature (optional)

1. Combine all of the slaw ingredients in a medium-size bowl. Cover and refrigerate until needed. (The slaw can be made up to 12 hours in advance.)

2. Fire up the grill for a two-level fire capable of cooking at the same time on both high heat (1 to 2 seconds with the hand test) and medium heat (4 to 5 seconds with the hand test); see page 6.

3. Grill the sausages, uncovered, for a total of 20 to 25 minutes. First cook the sausages over high heat for 8 to 10 minutes, rolling them every couple of minutes to crisp all sides. Move to medium heat and continue cooking for another 12 to 15 minutes, continuing to roll them. When done, the sausages should be brown, crisp, and thoroughly cooked, but still juicy. Toast the rolls on the edge of the grill if you wish.

4. Arrange the sausages in the toasted rolls, tuck a slice of cheese in at the side of each if you wish, and top with the slaw. Serve immediately.

THERE REALLY WAS AN OSCAR MAYER

A Bavarian immigrant, Oscar Mayer got his start in the meat business in 1873 at age 14 as a "butcher's boy" in Detroit. Over the next 10 years Oscar saved enough money to move to Chicago, the slaughterhouse capital of the country, and opened a meat market of his own. He focused at first on Old World sausages and Westphalian ham, but the young entrepreneur soon branched out to bacon and the product that was to turn him into a household name, the wiener. Fame came in the decades ahead through promotion of the skinless hot dog, the common kind today, and clever packaging that extended the shelf life of processed meat and provided opportunities for national distribution. A frank flair for publicity also helped. Oscar sold his dogs to butcher shops around Chicago out of a "wiener wagon," the first rendition of the now legendary Wienermobile.

FAJITAS, TACOS, AND OTHER SOUTH- WESTERN CLASSICS

TEXAS FAJITAS

Fajitas, both true and faux, became such popular fare in recent decades that it's hard to imagine that the skirt steak traditional to them was once just a lowly ranch ration. Mexican cowboys, or *vaqueros*, cooking on wood fires on the vast northern cattle ranges of their country, mastered the art of grilling the naturally tough but flavorful skirt, which they called *arracheras*. Immigrants brought the idea to the Southwest, where it evolved over time from a simple meat cook-out to the sizzling spread of beef, vegetables, and salsa we know today. Included here is the classic chunky fresh pico de gallo, but feel free to use another salsa if you prefer. **SERVES 4 TO 6**

MARINADE

Juice of 4 limes

1/4 cup Worcestershire sauce

2 tablespoons vegetable oil

2 to 3 pickled jalapeños, minced, plus 1/4 cup of the pickling liquid

6 garlic cloves, minced

2 skirt steaks (1 to 1¼ pounds each), trimmed of membrane and fat (if needed, cut into manageable sections of 9 to 12 inches)

About 8 metal or soaked bamboo skewers (optional)

1 to 2 medium-size onions, sliced thick

1 green bell pepper

1 red bell pepper

1 mild green chile, such as New Mexican or poblano

Vegetable oil

Kosher salt or coarse sea salt

PICO DE GALLO

3/4 pound red-ripe plum tomatoes, seeded and chopped

2 to 4 fresh or pickled jalapeños, seeded and minced

2 scallions, roots and limp green tops trimmed, sliced into thin rings

1/4 cup chopped white onion

1/4 cup chopped fresh cilantro

Juice of 1/2 lime

Kosher salt or coarse sea salt to taste

Small flour tortillas, warmed

Avocado slices

1. At least 2 1/2 hours and up to 24 hours before you plan to grill the fajitas, combine the marinade ingredients in a medium-size bowl. Place the skirt steaks in a zipper-top plastic bag and pour the marinade over them. Seal the bag, toss back and forth to distribute the marinade, and refrigerate.

2. If you wish, run a skewer horizontally through each onion slice to better hold the individual rings together. Coat the onion slices, bell peppers, and chile with oil. Drain the meat, discarding the marinade, and blot any moisture on the surface with a paper towel. Salt the meat lightly. Let the steaks sit at room temperature for about 30 minutes.

3. Mix up the pico de gallo ingredients in a small bowl.

4. Fire up the grill for a two-level fire capable of cooking at the same time on both high heat (1 to 2 seconds on the hand test) and medium heat (4 to 5 seconds with the same hand test); see page 6.

5. Place the skirt steaks over high heat and the onion slices, peppers, and chile over medium heat. Grill the steaks, uncovered, 4 to 5 minutes per side for medium-rare. Turn them a minimum of three times, more often if juices begin to pool on the surface. Let the steaks rest for 5 to 10 minutes before slicing them. The total cooking time for the onions, peppers, and chile will be 8 to 18 minutes, until the onions are soft and the peppers and chile are soft and have some charred skins. Turn the onion slices at least once and the peppers and chile several times, to cook on all sides evenly. While

the vegetables finish cooking, cut the skirt steaks diagonally across the grain into thin finger-length strips. As soon as the peppers and chile come off the grill, transfer them to a plastic or paper bag and close it to let them steam, loosening the skin. Pull the charred skin off the peppers and chile, seed them, and slice them into strips.

6. To serve, pile a platter high with the meat, onions, peppers, and chile. Accompany with warm tortillas, avocado slices, and the pico de gallo. Let everyone help themselves by filling the tortillas with some of the skirt steak strips, vegetables, and garnishes.

THE BIRTH OF THE GRILL

The country's first book on grilling, *Sunset's Barbecue Book* from 1938, dealt with food and cooking only as a secondary interest. Most of the slender volume concerned how to build your own outdoor fireplace grill, using brick, rock, and mortar. It seemed a natural, woodsy fixture in a suburban backyard, particularly in sunny regions of the West, where grilling gained its initial foothold in the nation.

By 1942, another early grilling book noted—after a lengthy review of wood-burning fireplace grills—that "the growing popularity of charcoal for outdoor cooking has acted as a real incentive for what you might call 'mass production' of various appliances designed for the use of this fuel. Almost every hardware store carries them and there seem to be more models and makes of charcoal stoves than automobiles." The book pictured two styles, neither very recognizable as an ancestor of the modern metal grill.

Simple charcoal braziers and hibachis hit the market within a few years, and the first covered grills didn't lag far behind. Tulsa pioneer Grant Hastings brought out his innovative Hasty-Bake in 1948, though he had a hard time selling it in the early days because of the hood, widely viewed as an unnecessary frill. George Stephen had more success with the covered Weber kettle, introduced in 1951, which established a design and a company that still dominate the industry. At the time, total grill sales barely topped 250,000 a year, but they shot up to over five million annually by 1965. These days, yearly sales average $15 million.

DRUNKEN FAJITAS

Fajitas are such a perfect grill food for family meals as well as entertaining that we feel everyone should have a couple of versions in their repertoire. This one gets a two-step prep prior to cooking. The meat soaks in a beer and citrus mixture and then is massaged with a dry rub of chili powder and brown sugar. To keep the surface of the meat crusty, we forego traditional accompanying grilled vegetables, but we do like a few avocado slices tucked into each fajita. **SERVES 4 TO 6**

BEER MARINADE

12 ounces (1^1/2 cups) beer

Juice of 1 orange

Juice of 3 limes

2 tablespoons Worcestershire sauce

2 skirt steaks (1 to 1^1/4 pounds each), trimmed of membrane and fat (if needed, cut into manageable sections of 9 to 12 inches)

DRY RUB

1 tablespoon chili powder

1 tablespoon kosher salt or coarse sea salt

1 tablespoon packed brown sugar

1^1/2 teaspoons ground cumin

Small flour tortillas, warmed

Pico de Gallo (page 79) or other favorite salsa

Avocado slices

1. At least 2^1/2 hours and up to 24 hours before you plan to grill the fajitas, combine the marinade ingredients in a medium-size bowl. Place the skirt steaks in a zipper-top plastic bag and pour the marinade over them. Seal the bag, toss back and forth to distribute the marinade, and refrigerate.

2. Drain the steaks, discarding the marinade, and blot any moisture on the surface with a paper towel. Combine the dry rub ingredients in a small bowl. Coat the steaks with the rub and let them sit, covered, at room temperature for about 30 minutes.

3. Fire up the grill, bringing the temperature to high (1 to 2 seconds with the hand test).

4. Grill the steaks, uncovered, for 4 to 5 minutes per side, to medium-rare doneness. The steaks should be turned a minimum of three times, more often if juices begin to pool on the surface. Let the steaks rest for 5 to 10 minutes before slicing.

5. Cut the steaks diagonally across the grain into thin finger-length strips. To serve, pile a platter high with the hot meat and accompany with the warm tortillas, salsa, and avocado slices. Let everyone help themselves by filling the tortillas with some of the skirt steak and portions of the garnishes.

the meat soaks in a beer and citrus mixture and then is massaged with a dry rub of chili powder and brown sugar

CUMIN-RUBBED CARNE ASADA

Carne asada means "roasted meat" in Spanish, but in the Southwest it almost always refers to grilled steak. Different cooks use various cuts of beef, but we prefer either center-cut (eye of) chuck or the newer chuck cut, flatiron steak. Since the steak is traditionally served thin, the chuck will be cut into 1/2-inch-thick slices. It grills best over moderate heat to a juicy medium doneness. Because the cumin is so essential to the taste of the dish, the rub starts with seeds for you to toast and grind yourself for maximum flavor potency. Serve with limes, the tomatillo salsa, and *cebollitas,* which are small onions on the stem. **SERVES 4**

TOMATILLO SALSA

3/4 pound fresh tomatillos, husks removed

1/3 cup chopped white onion

1/4 cup lightly packed fresh cilantro leaves

2 serrano chiles or 1 or 2 jalapeños, stemmed and, if you wish, seeded

1 tablespoon fresh lime juice, or more to taste

1 tablespoon vegetable oil

1/2 teaspoon kosher salt or coarse sea salt, or more to taste

1/4 teaspoon ground cumin

CUMIN DRY RUB

1 tablespoon cumin seeds, toasted in a dry skillet over medium heat until fragrant, then ground in a spice grinder or with a mortar and pestle

2 tablespoons kosher salt or coarse sea salt

8 large scallions or baby bulb onions on the stem, roots and limp tops trimmed

2 limes, cut lengthwise into 6 wedges each

Vegetable oil

2 pounds eye of chuck, preferably, or other chuck or flatiron steak, cut across the grain into 1/2-inch-thick slices

1. Puree the salsa ingredients in a blender. Taste and adjust the amount of lime juice or salt, if you wish. Refrigerate until serving time.

2. Mix together the dry rub ingredients in a small bowl.

3. Fire up the grill, bringing the temperature to medium (4 to 5 seconds with the hand test).

4. Coat the scallions and lime wedges with oil.

5. Pound the meat slices lightly with the smooth side of a meat pounder to a thickness of 1/4 to 1/3 inch. They'll be kind of tattered and unpromising looking.

6. Place the meat on the grill and tuck the scallions and limes around the meat. Grill the meat, uncovered, for 10 to 12 minutes, turning it at least 3 times and sprinkling it with the rub each time. Turn more often if juices begin to pool on the surface. When done, the meat should be glistening and well browned (not gray-brown) on the surface with very little, if any, hint of pink at the center. Turn the scallions and limes occasionally, taking them off the grill when they are soft and have a bit of char in spots.

7. For each portion, pile several meat slices on top of each other or at least overlapping on each plate. Top with a couple of grilled scallions and lime wedges and serve hot, with the salsa passed on the side.

GRILLING TIP

For a festive Mexican meal, turn carne asada into the centerpiece of a vibrant Tampiqueña platter, the country's only significant "combo" plate. Add a simple version of a cheese enchilada and slices of grilled mild chiles, such as poblanos. Fill out the plates with rice and refried beans. "Tampiqueña" indicates that the meal is from Tampico, but it reportedly originated at a club by that name in Mexico City.

CHUCK STEAK TACOS

Long before the world's first fast-food taco, tortillas were soft and beef fillings were shredded, as in this robust version. Eye of chuck has long been favored for the beef, but the newer flatiron steak cut offers similar full meaty flavor.

SERVES 4

MARINADE

1/4 cup vegetable oil

2 tablespoons pickling liquid from a jar of pickled jalapeños

2 tablespoons fresh lime juice

1 1/2 teaspoons cumin seeds, toasted in a dry skillet over medium heat until fragrant, then ground

1 1/2 teaspoons chili powder

3 garlic cloves, minced

1 1/2 pounds eye of chuck or other chuck or flatiron steak, cut across the grain into 1/2-inch-thick slices

CHIPOTLE SALSA

3/4 pound red-ripe plum tomatoes

1/2 medium-size onion, cut into chunks

3 tablespoons chopped fresh cilantro

2 tablespoons distilled white or cider vinegar, or more to taste

2 to 3 canned chipotle chiles in adobo, plus 1 to 2 teaspoons adobo sauce

2 garlic cloves, chopped

1 teaspoon kosher salt or coarse sea salt, or more to taste

Kosher salt or coarse sea salt

Minced onion and fresh cilantro (optional)

12 or more soft corn tortillas, warmed

Shredded lettuce and grated mild cheddar cheese or crumbled *queso fresco*

1. At least 4 hours and up to 24 hours before you plan to grill the meat, combine the marinade ingredients in a small bowl.

2. Pound the chuck slices lightly with the smooth side of a meat pounder to a thickness of 1/4 inch. Place the rather sorry-looking meat in a zipper-top plastic bag and pour the marinade over it. Seal the bag, toss back and forth to distribute the marinade, and refrigerate. Turn occasionally if the meat isn't thoroughly submerged in the marinade.

3. While the meat marinates, prepare the salsa. If you have a gas grill, fire it up to high heat (1 to 2 seconds with the hand test). Otherwise, heat the oven broiler. Place the tomatoes on a small baking sheet if broiling. Broil the tomatoes for 15 to 18 minutes, turning occasionally, until they are soft and the skins split and turn dark in many spots. If using the grill, place the tomatoes on the cooking grate and cook for a similar amount of time, turning occasionally. Once done, puree the tomatoes with their skins and cores in a blender with the remaining salsa ingredients. Use warm or refrigerate if not using within the hour. (The salsa tastes best the day it's made but can be kept for another day.)

4. Drain the meat, discarding the marinade, and let it sit, covered, at room temperature for about 30 minutes.

5. Fire up the grill, bringing the temperature to medium (4 to 5 seconds with the hand test).

6. Grill the meat, uncovered, for about 10 minutes. Turn at least 3 times, or more often if juices begin to pool on the surface. When done, the meat should be glistening and well browned (not gray-brown) on the surface with very little, if any, hint of pink at the center. Shred the meat with your fingers. Add salt to taste and, if you wish, some onion or cilantro, or both, to make the taco filling.

7. Serve the taco filling with the warm tortillas, salsa, lettuce, and cheese heaped on a platter or in separate bowls. Let everyone fill each of their tortillas with several tablespoons of filling, and top with the remaining ingredients.

CHIPOTLE CHICKEN TACOS

Chicken and the smoky chipotle chile make a zippy pairing. A creamy lime sauce joins the duo in place of salsa for a tangy finish. Pound the chicken thin so that it has lots of crusty edges when shredded. We like these served in crunchy taco shells, but opt for soft corn tortillas if you prefer. **SERVES 4**

CHIPOTLE MARINADE

1/4 cup plus 2 tablespoons vegetable oil

1/4 cup fresh orange or tangerine juice

1 tablespoon fresh lime juice

1 to 2 minced canned chipotle chiles in adobo and 1 tablespoon adobo sauce or 2 tablespoons chipotle ketchup

1 garlic clove, minced

Kosher salt or coarse sea salt

Freshly ground black pepper

4 medium-size boneless, skinless chicken breast halves, pounded to a thickness of 1/4 inch

3 to 4 medium-size limes, each cut lengthwise into 4 wedges

Vegetable oil

LIME SAUCE

1/2 cup mayonnaise

1/2 cup sour cream

2 tablespoons minced fresh cilantro

1 tablespoon fresh lime juice

1/4 to 1/2 teaspoon ground dried green chile or green chile seasoning, or minced pickled jalapeño to taste

12 taco shells

1. At least 1 hour and up to 24 hours before you plan to grill, whisk together the marinade ingredients in a small bowl. Place the pounded chicken breasts in a zipper-top plastic bag and pour in the marinade. Seal the bag, toss back and forth to coat evenly, and refrigerate.

2. Shortly before you plan to grill, place the lime quarters on a small plate. Rub them lightly with oil and set aside at room temperature.

3. Stir together the lime sauce ingredients in a small bowl. Refrigerate until ready to serve.

4. Drain the chicken and discard the marinade. Let the chicken sit, uncovered, at room temperature for about 20 minutes.

5. Fire up the grill, bringing the temperature to medium (4 to 5 seconds with the hand test).

6. Grill the chicken, uncovered, for 6 to 8 minutes total, until white throughout but still juicy. Turn three times, rotating the breasts a half turn each time to get crisscross grill marks. Grill the limes alongside the chicken, turning from time to time so that they soften and develop a bit of char. Remove the limes as they are done.

7. Working quickly, pull the chicken into thin shreds and pile it on a platter, surrounded by the limes and taco shells and accompanied by the sauce. Serve immediately, encouraging diners to fill the shells, drizzle with sauce, squeeze on the warm lime juice, and enjoy.

SANTA BARBARA FISH TACOS

It took the Baja peninsula's fish tacos a little longer than beef to catch on with American audiences, but there aren't many doubters left today. We became early advocates on our first visit to Santa Barbara years ago, and the tacos have been on our top 100 list ever since then. The fish in many Baja tacos is fried, but grilling gives a great result, complete with some crispy edges. **SERVES 4**

2 cups chopped romaine or other sturdy lettuce

2 small red-ripe plum tomatoes, chopped

3 tablespoons minced red onion

2 tablespoons minced fresh cilantro

3 limes, halved

2 pounds white fish fillets, such as snapper, mahi mahi, or sea bass

1 tablespoon extra-virgin olive oil

2 garlic cloves, minced

Kosher salt or coarse sea salt

Freshly ground black pepper

16 thin corn tortillas, warmed

A favorite salsa, such as Chipotle Salsa (page 86)

Avocado slices

1. Just before you plan to fire up the grill, mix the lettuce, tomatoes, onion, and cilantro together in a medium-size bowl with the juice of half a lime. Cover and refrigerate until serving time.

2. Squeeze the remaining lime juice over the fish, rub the fillets with the oil and garlic, and sprinkle them lightly with salt and pepper.

3. Fire up the grill, bringing the temperature to medium-high to high (2 to 3 seconds with the hand test).

4. Transfer the fillets to a well-oiled cooking grate or, preferably, to a hinged grill basket or well-oiled small-mesh grill rack placed on the cooking grate. Grill, uncovered, for 4 to 5 minutes per 1/2 inch of thickness, turning once. The fish is done when flaky and opaque.

5. Break the fish into bite-size pieces. To assemble a taco, place 1 tortilla on top of a second tortilla. (This makes a stronger base for what will be a large taco.) Spoon on several heaping tablespoons of the fish, then top with the salad garnish, salsa, and avocado slices. Eat immediately.

grilling gives fish tacos a great result, complete with some crispy edges

FLAME-KISSED CHILE RELLENOS

A chile relleno is usually fried in a heavy batter. We prefer to grill them, which accentuates the fruity flavor of the chiles, and then serve them with a sprightly cilantro sauce. **SERVES 4**

CHEESE FILLING

8 ounces Chihuahua or Muenster cheese, grated

6 ounces creamy fresh goat cheese or cream cheese, or a combination, softened

1/2 cup fresh or (thawed) frozen corn kernels

1/4 cup pine nuts, toasted in a dry skillet over medium heat until golden

2 tablespoons minced onion

CILANTRO SAUCE

3/4 cup chopped fresh cilantro

1/2 to 1 jalapeño or serrano chile

3/4 cup Mexican *crema* (or substitute crème fraîche or sour cream)

1/8 teaspoon kosher salt or coarse sea salt

8 meaty medium-size poblano chiles or other fresh, fat mild green chiles such as New Mexican or Anaheim

Vegetable oil spray

Chopped tomato (optional)

1. Mix together the filling ingredients in a medium-size bowl. Cover and chill until needed. (The filling can be made up to 1 day in advance.)

2. To prepare the cilantro sauce, combine the cilantro and jalapeño in a food processor and process until very finely minced. Spoon in the *crema* and salt and process again until well blended. Cover and refrigerate until needed. (The sauce can be made up to 2 hours ahead, but the cilantro's sparkle and vibrancy will begin to fade after that point.)

3. Fire up the grill, bringing the temperature to medium (4 to 5 seconds with the hand test).

4. Grill the chiles, uncovered, for 8 to 10 minutes, turning occasionally so that the skin blackens and blisters all over. Place the chiles in a plastic bag to steam as they cool.

5. When the chiles are cool enough to handle, peel them, wearing rubber gloves if your skin is sensitive. Slit each chile from end to end on one side only and remove any loose seeds. Don't remove the seed pod or it will weaken the walls of the chile. (The chiles can be prepared to this point 1 day ahead, covered, and refrigerated. Bring them back to room temperature before proceeding.)

6. Stuff (but don't overstuff) the cheese mixture into the chiles, bringing the slit edges of each chile back together tightly. If you can't get the edges to stick back together, re-move some of the cheese. Spritz the chiles with oil. Return the chiles to the grill, slit side down. Grill, uncovered, for about 2 minutes, then carefully roll the chiles over onto their opposite sides and grill for 3 to 5 minutes more. When ready, the chiles will have a few charred marks and the cheese will be heated through and gooey.

7. Serve the chiles hot, with a drizzle of the sauce.

grilling them accentuates the fruity flavor of the chiles

SIZZLING STEAKS, CHOPS, AND RIBS

A PORTERHOUSE FROM HEAVEN

When Mark Twain traveled in Europe in the 1870s, he concluded that Old World chefs knew nothing about steaks. Confronted one day by a cut that he called an "inert thing," he fantasized about "an angel suddenly sweeping down out of a better land" with "a mighty porter-house steak an inch and a half thick, hot and sputtering from the griddle." We illustrate his point in this simply seasoned prime-grade porterhouse, the American steak lover's favorite cut since the days of the first rowdy New York City chop houses. **SERVES 4 TO 6**

> Two 1¹/2-inch-thick prime porterhouse steaks (about 2 pounds each), preferably dry aged
>
> Kosher salt or coarse sea salt
>
> Freshly ground black pepper
>
> 4 tablespoons (¹/2 stick) highest-quality, freshest butter you can locate, cut into 4 pats, at room temperature

1. Generously sprinkle the steaks with salt and pepper and let them sit, covered, at room temperature for 30 to 45 minutes.

2. Fire up the grill for a two-level fire capable of cooking at the same time on both high heat (1 to 2 seconds with the hand test) and medium heat (4 to 5 seconds with the hand test); see page 6.

3. Grill the steaks, uncovered, over high heat for 2¹/2 to 3 minutes per side. Move the steaks to medium heat, turning them again, and continue grilling for 3 to 4 minutes per side for medium-rare. While grilling over medium, keep the smaller, more tender section of the porterhouses angled away from the fire a bit. The steaks should be turned a minimum of three times, more often if juices begin to pool on the surface. Rotate a half turn each time for crisscross grill marks. Transfer to a platter and immediately top each with 2 pats of butter. Let the steaks rest for 5 to 10 minutes.

4. Bring the steaks to the table, slice the meat from the bones in thin strips, and serve hot, making sure to spoon the mingling meat juices and butter from the platter onto each portion.

FIRED-UP STEAK

Serious meat loves serious heat. The first step in transforming a fine steak into a memorable meal is searing the surface of the meat quickly over a blazing charcoal fire or a fully cranked-up gas grill. The trick is knowing when and how to cut back the heat to prevent burning the meat.

For superior steaks an inch or more in thickness—cuts such as porterhouse, T-bone, strip, and rib-eye—we suggest a two-level fire capable of cooking on both very high heat (1 to 2 seconds or less with the hand test) and medium heat (4 to 5 seconds with the hand test). Sear the steaks well on each side over high and then move them to medium heat to cook the center through to the desired doneness. You make the temperature transition earlier in some cases than others, as with lean tenderloin medallions that dry out fast over high heat. On the other hand, some thinner, less tender cuts, such as skirt and hanger steaks, thrive over the hot fire and don't need any time at a lower level to cook through. Because buffalo and venison steaks are especially lean, they should never be grilled beyond medium-rare, which is our strong preference for beef steaks, too.

Before grilling, take the chill off all meat. Given current knowledge about the possibility of bacterial contamination, we don't recommend bringing meat fully to room temperature in a home kitchen, but it should sit out for a short spell before going onto the grill to make sure you don't end up with a cold center. To promote even cooking, we turn steaks at least three times, so that each side gets two periods of direct exposure to the fire.

CARPETBAG STEAK

This American classic is the ultimate surf-and-turf dish, a delectable sirloin strip steak stuffed with fresh briny oysters. It's a treat you're bound to repeat. **SERVES 4**

DRY RUB

2½ teaspoons celery salt

1½ teaspoons sweet paprika

1½ teaspoons freshly ground black pepper

1½ teaspoons ground white pepper

¾ teaspoon dried crumbled thyme

Two 1- to 1¼-inch-thick boneless sirloin strip steaks (14 to 16 ounces each), with a horizontal pocket cut into each one for stuffing

⅓ to ½ cup shucked oysters

1. At least 2 hours and up to 12 hours before you plan to grill the steaks, combine the dry rub ingredients in a small bowl. Set aside 1 teaspoon of the dry rub. Massage the steaks well with the remaining mixture inside and out. Cover the steaks and refrigerate them.

2. Remove the steaks from the refrigerator and let them sit at room temperature for about 30 minutes. Drain the oysters gently. Toss the oysters with the remaining 1 teaspoon rub and stuff half of the oysters into each steak.

3. Fire up the grill for a two-level fire capable of cooking at the same time on both high heat (1 to 2 seconds with the hand test) and medium heat (4 to 5 seconds with the hand test); see page 6.

4. Grill the steaks, uncovered, over high heat for 2½ to 3 minutes per side. Move them to medium heat, turning them again, and continue grilling for 2½ to 3 minutes per side for medium-rare doneness. Rotate a half turn each time for crisscross grill marks. Turn the steaks a minimum of three times, but more often if juices begin to pool on the surface.

5. Cut the steaks in half to create 4 portions, and serve.

STEPHAN PYLES' TEXAS RIB-EYE

We've eaten at many great steakhouses, but we've never had a better steak than the chile-crusted gem that Stephan Pyles used to serve at his former Star Canyon in Dallas. The soft-spoken but outgoing chef, who kindly provided us with his recipe, attributed its success to using prime Texas beef, a roaring hickory fire for grilling, and a robust dry rub. The exuberantly seasoned onion rings were part and parcel of the steak at Star Canyon, and moderately easy to manage on a grill with a side burner, but you won't go hungry or unsatisfied without them. Stephan accompanied the steak with a wonderfully complex mixture of wild mushrooms and pinto beans. At home, we go simpler, marinating some portobello slices in extra steak rub and cooking them alongside the meat on medium heat. This is splurge eating at its finest. **SERVES 4 OR MORE**

COWBOY RUB

1/4 cup smoked sweet paprika

1/4 cup ground dried medium-hot red chiles, such as a mixture of guajillo, pasilla, and chipotle

2 tablespoons kosher salt or coarse sea salt

1 tablespoon plus 1 teaspoon sugar

Four 1 1/4- to 1 1/2-inch-thick bone-in rib-eye steaks (1 1/4 to 1 1/2 pounds each), at least choice grade and preferably prime grade

RED CHILE ONION RINGS

3 medium-size onions, cut into 1/4-inch-thick slices

Milk

1 cup all-purpose flour

1/4 cup smoked sweet paprika

1/4 cup ground dried medium-hot red chiles, such as a mixture of guajillo, pasilla, and chipotle

1/4 cup ground cumin

Kosher salt or coarse sea salt to taste

Cayenne pepper (optional)

Vegetable oil for deep-frying

1. At least 2 1/2 hours and up to 12 hours before you plan to grill the steaks, combine the dry rub ingredients in a small bowl. Coat the steaks thickly with the mixture. Cover the steaks and refrigerate.

2. About an hour before you plan to grill the steaks, get the onion rings ready for frying. Place the onion slices in a large bowl and cover them with milk. In a clean paper or plastic bag, combine the flour, paprika, ground chiles, cumin, salt, and, if you wish, a few pinches of cayenne for additional zing. Pour at least 4 inches of oil in a Dutch oven or other large, heavy pot.

3. Remove the steaks from the refrigerator and let them sit at room temperature for about 30 minutes.

4. Fire up the grill for a two-level fire capable of cooking at the same time both high heat (1 to 2 seconds with the hand test) and medium heat (4 to 5 seconds with the hand test); see page 6.

5. Grill the steaks, uncovered, over high heat for 3 to 3 1/2 minutes per side. Move them to medium heat, turning them again, and continue grilling for 2 1/2 to 3 minutes per side for medium-rare. Rotate a half turn each time for crisscross grill marks. The steaks should be turned a minimum of three times, more often if juices begin to pool on the surface.

6. Meanwhile, heat the oil for the onion rings to 375°F. Drain the onions and dredge them in the seasoned flour. Fry the onions, in batches, for 2 to 3 minutes, until crisp. Transfer to a rack.

7. Serve the steaks right away, with portions of the hot onion rings piled high on top of the meat.

A bone-in rib-eye is a grand cut, essentially a hearty slab of the prime rib. (Just to be confusing, a prime rib isn't necessarily USDA prime grade.) If your market has only boneless rib-eye, it won't look quite so dramatic but can be grilled in the same fashion.

the chef uses prime Texas beef, a roaring hickory fire for grilling, and a robust dry rub

FLORENTINE T-BONE

When you order a *bistecca alla fiorentina* in Italy, the kitchen is likely to send out a giant T-bone or porterhouse for your inspection before the cooking begins, to get your assent to the quality and size of the cut. The chef seasons the meat simply, grills it over hot wood coals, tops it with fine olive oil, and often serves the steak on a bed of peppery arugula fresh from the garden. **SERVES 4 OR MORE**

Four 1¼- to 1½-inch-thick T-bone steaks (1 to 1¼ pounds), at least choice grade

Kosher salt or coarse sea salt

Freshly ground black pepper

4 to 6 cups arugula

Top-quality extra-virgin olive oil

Lemon wedges, for serving

1. Generously sprinkle the steaks with salt and pepper and let them sit, covered, at room temperature for 30 to 45 minutes.

2. Fire up the grill for a two-level fire capable of cooking at the same time on both high heat (1 to 2 seconds with the hand test) and medium heat (4 to 5 seconds with the hand test); see page 6.

3. Grill the steaks, uncovered, over high heat for 2½ to 3 minutes per side. Move the steaks to medium heat, turning them again, and continue grilling for 2½ to 3 minutes per side for medium-rare. While grilling over medium, keep the smaller, more tender section of the T-bones angled away from the fire a bit. The steaks should be turned a minimum of three times, more often if juices begin to pool on the surface. Rotate a half turn each time for crisscross grill marks.

4. Transfer the steaks to plates, with the arugula under, over, or on the side, as you wish. Immediately drizzle enough oil over the top of each steak to make it glisten, with little rivers of oil barely pooling on the sides. Accompany with lemons for squeezing over the meat.

MUSTARD-RUBBED BISON STEAK

American bison steaks come in the same cuts as beef, but are likely to be both a bit smaller and a lot pricier. To avoid overcooking the lean, always grass-fed meat, pay extra close attention to the cooking time and the fire's heat. **SERVES 4 OR MORE**

2 tablespoons yellow mustard

2 teaspoons freshly ground black pepper

2 teaspoons Worcestershire sauce

1 teaspoon crumbled dried sage, or more to taste

Four 1-inch-thick strip, rib-eye, or sirloin buffalo steaks (8 to 10 ounces each)

Kosher salt or coarse sea salt

1. Mix the mustard, pepper, Worcestershire, and sage in a small bowl. Rub the mixture over the buffalo steaks. Generously sprinkle the steaks with salt and let them sit, covered, at room temperature for 20 to 30 minutes.

2. Fire up a grill for a two-level fire capable of cooking at the same time on both high heat (1 to 2 seconds with the hand test) and medium heat (4 to 5 seconds with the hand test); see page 6.

3. Grill the steaks, uncovered, over high heat for about 2 minutes per side. Move the steaks to medium heat, turning them again, and continue grilling for 2 to 2 1/2 minutes per side for medium-rare. The steaks should be turned a minimum of three times, more often if juices begin to pool on the surface. Rotate a half turn each time for crisscross grill marks. Serve immediately.

PICKAPEPPA-MARINATED FLANK STEAK

Flank has great beefy flavor, but to get there, you have to tame its tough side. The key to success is a combination of quick cooking and thin slicing against the grain. We marinate it here with Jamaican Pickapeppa sauce, a tangy bottled seasoning based on tamarind. You'll find it in your supermarket near the steak sauce. **SERVES 6**

Two 1^1/$_4$-pound flank steaks

MARINADE
^{1}/$_2$ cup Pickapeppa sauce

^{1}/$_4$ cup soy sauce

^{1}/$_4$ cup Worcestershire sauce

3 tablespoons red wine vinegar

2 tablespoons packed dark brown sugar

2 garlic cloves, minced

1. Place the steaks in a shallow nonreactive pan in a single layer. Whisk together the marinade ingredients in a small bowl. Pour the marinade over the steaks, cover, and refrigerate for at least 8 hours and up to 24 hours. Turn the steaks occasionally.

2. Fire up the grill for a two-level fire capable of cooking at the same time on both high heat (1 to 2 seconds with the hand test) and medium heat (4 to 5 seconds with the hand test); see page 6.

3. Remove the steaks from the marinade, reserving the liquid.

4. Grill the steaks, uncovered, over high heat for 2^1/$_2$ to 3 minutes per side. Move the steaks to medium heat, turning them again, and continue grilling for 2^1/$_2$ to 3 minutes per side for medium-rare. The steaks should be turned a minimum of three times, more often if juices begin to pool on the surface. Rotate a half turn each time for crisscross grill marks.

5. Bring the marinade to a full boil in a small saucepan, reducing it by about a third, a matter of just a few minutes. Slice the steaks thinly across the grain and drizzle with the reduced marinade. Serve right away.

TO DRESS A BEEF-STAKE, SUFFICIENT FOR TWO GENTLEMEN, WITH A FIRE MADE OF TWO NEWSPAPERS

Under that long recipe title, Amelia Simmons gave us the secret to a Colonial American steak. In the first cookbook written in this country, her 1796 *American Cookery*, Simmons instructed readers to put slices of beef in a pewter platter, cover the meat with water, add salt and pepper, and place another platter on top. Then, she said, sit "your dish upon a stool bottom upwards, the legs of such length as to raise the platter three inches from the board; cut your newspaper into small strips, light with a candle and apply them gradually, so as to keep a live fire under the whole dish." When you've burned two newspapers, the steak is done and "butter may then be applied, so as to render it grateful." And grateful we are as well for the modern grill.

ELK BACKSTRAP MEDALLIONS WITH PURPLE ONIONS AND PLUM SAUCE

In the venison universe—elk, antelope, caribou, deer—the backstrap is the equivalent of the beef tenderloin, so expect it to be priced accordingly unless you hunt your own or are tight with someone who does. As with beef from this mostly unused muscle, the meltingly tender meat, cut into medallions here, can always use a bit of a boost in the flavor department. Though the recipe calls for elk, any venison backstrap medallions will work. We owe the idea for this preparation to Abby Fisher, the earliest known African-American cookbook author. In *What Mrs. Fisher Knows about Old Southern Cooking* (1881), she suggests grilling venison steaks (i.e., "broiling" over hot coals on a gridiron) and provides the original version of the accompanying "game sauce." If you lack enough grill space to cook the elk medallions and onion slices simultaneously, make a two-level fire and grill the onions first over medium heat and then grill the elk, using both levels of heat. **SERVES 4**

PLUM SAUCE

1/3 cup minced onion

1/2 cup cider vinegar or other fruit vinegar

1 pound ripe plums, pitted and quartered, with their juice

1/2 cup sugar, or more to taste

One 1-inch piece cinnamon stick

1/4 teaspoon kosher salt or coarse sea salt, or more to taste

1/4 teaspoon freshly ground black pepper

Scant 1/4 teaspoon cayenne pepper

Eight 1- to 1^1/4-inch-thick elk or other venison backstrap medallions (4 to 5 ounces each; see Grilling Tip on page 108)

Kosher salt or coarse sea salt

Freshly ground black pepper

Vegetable oil

1 large red onion, cut into 1/3-inch-thick slices

About 8 metal or soaked bamboo skewers (optional)

1 to 2 tablespoons unsalted butter, cut into small chunks and softened

1. To prepare the plum sauce, combine the onion and vinegar in a medium-size saucepan, cover, and sweat over low heat until the onion has softened, about 5 minutes. Add the remaining ingredients, raise the heat to medium, and continue to cook, stirring occasionally, until reduced to jam consistency, about another 30 minutes. Taste and, if needed, add a few more teaspoons of sugar or a few more pinches of salt, and cook another minute or two. (The sauce can be made a day ahead, refrigerated, and served chilled or reheated. If it is too thick for easy spooning, whisk in a bit of water.)

2. Fire up a grill for a two-level fire capable of cooking at the same time on both high heat (1 to 2 seconds with the hand test) and medium heat (4 to 5 seconds with the hand test); see page 6.

3. Sprinkle the elk medallions with salt and pepper to taste. Wrap them tightly in plastic and let them sit at room temperature for about 20 minutes. If you wish, run a skewer through each onion slice to make it easier to keep the rings together while cooking. Oil the onion slices and season with salt and pepper.

4. Plan on a total cooking time for the elk of 9 to 11 minutes, and for the onions, closer to 15 minutes. Place the onion slices on the grill first over medium heat and grill, uncovered, for 6 to 8 minutes. Turn the onions and place the elk on the grill over high heat. Grill the elk, uncovered, for 1 to 1^1/2 minutes per side. Move the medallions to medium heat, turning them again, and continue grilling for 2 to 3 minutes per side, for rare to medium-rare doneness. Rotate a half turn each time the medallions are turned over for crisscross grill marks.

5. Take off the onions and elk as each is done, arranging them on a platter and dotting them with a bit of butter. Keep the platter loosely tented with foil while everything finishes cooking. Serve immediately with spoonfuls of the plum sauce.

GRILLING TIP

Venison backstrap is sometimes sold just in thin slices or scallops, especially if from deer or caribou, which are smaller than elk. If that's the way you find it, you'll need to modify the grilling technique slightly. Cook the onion slices over the medium-heat side of the grill first. Then cook the venison scallops just over high heat and for only 1 to 1½ minutes per side.

CHURCH-PICNIC PORK CHOPS

Bill grew up in Texas, where they put dry rubs on baby food, but Cheryl had no knowledge of the flavoring technique in Illinois until she attended a church picnic as a teenager. One of the cooks dressed his pork chops with a basic blend of dry spices, rubbing the homemade mixture into the meat before cooking. In an era of plain foods and commercialized condiments, the intensity of the taste and the crispness of the coating was an epiphany for Cheryl as an aspiring cook. We recapture that early rapture in these simple bone-in chops, though our rub today is a little more devilish than the original. **SERVES 4**

CHILE DRY RUB

2 tablespoons sweet paprika

1 tablespoon kosher salt or coarse sea salt

1 tablespoon ground chipotle chile

1 tablespoon ground dried mild to medium-hot red chile, such as New Mexican, ancho, or pasilla, or a combination of these chiles

1 teaspoon ground cumin

3/4 teaspoon sugar

Four 3/4-inch-thick bone-in center-cut pork chops (10 to 11 ounces each)

Vegetable oil spray

A favorite barbecue sauce (optional)

1. At least 2 hours and up to 8 hours before you plan to grill the pork chops, combine the dry rub ingredients in a small bowl. Coat the chops with the spice mixture, place them in a zipper-top plastic bag, and refrigerate.

2. Fire up the grill, bringing the temperature to medium (4 to 5 seconds with the hand test).

3. Remove the chops from the refrigerator and let them sit at room temperature for about 20 minutes.

4. Spritz the chops with oil and transfer them to the grill. Grill, uncovered, for 20 to 23 minutes, turning three times while cooking. Rotate the chops a half turn each time for crisscross grill marks. The chops are done when barely white at the center with clear juices. (Don't confuse the colors of the dry rub and the juices.)

5. Serve the chops hot, with barbecue sauce on the side, if you wish.

GRILLING PORK

One of the oldest domesticated animals on earth—right after dogs—hogs have provided many centuries of great eating. The bounty doesn't always reach the grill, however. Outside the Midwest at least, pork often takes a back seat to beef and chicken on American backyard menus.

Now a much leaner meat than in the past, but still a hearty partner for a broad range of spices and other seasonings, pork presents a wealth of potential. A number of different cuts grill easily and well, affording variety in taste and texture, and even the tough, fire-resistant ribs make a magnificent meal with a little extra effort.

Our only caution is to watch the heat so you don't scorch the meat. In general, pork grills best on a medium fire, which crusts the surface slowly to allow thorough cooking of the interior. You want a just-white center with clear juices, measuring 155° to 160°F on an instant-read meat thermometer. Tenderloin is an exception to the rule about heat; it thrives on a two-level fire, searing quickly on high before finishing on medium. It's also exceptional in flavor compared to many foods, but only one of several pork cuts that make us want to pig out grandly on the grill.

CUBAN-STYLE PORK TENDERLOIN

Cuban cooks often season pork with *mojo*, a sauce based on garlic, olive oil, and citrus juice, traditionally sour orange juice. We love the robust flavor it contributes to tenderloin. Since sour oranges are difficult to find in most areas of this country, we substitute a combination of juice from regular oranges and limes. **SERVES 4**

MOJO MARINADE AND SAUCE
Juice of 3 large oranges (about 1^1/2 cups)
Juice of 2 large limes
6 tablespoons extra-virgin olive oil
^{1}/3 cup minced fresh flat-leaf parsley
2 tablespoons minced fresh oregano
1 teaspoon kosher salt or coarse sea salt
2 plump garlic cloves, minced

Two 12- to 14-ounce pork tenderloins
Avocado slices and red-ripe tomato slices, for garnish

1. At least 2^1/2 hours and up to 24 hours before you plan to grill the pork, mix the *mojo* ingredients in a small bowl. Set aside one-third of the *mojo* for the sauce; cover and refrigerate. Place the tenderloins in a zipper-top plastic bag and pour the remaining two-thirds of the *mojo* over them. Seal the bag, toss back and forth to distribute the marinade, and refrigerate.

2. Drain the pork, discarding the marinade, and blot any excess moisture on the surface with a paper towel. Let the pork sit, covered, at room temperature for 20 to 30 minutes.

3. Fire up the grill for a two-level fire capable of cooking at the same time on both high heat (1 to 2 seconds with the hand test) and medium heat (4 to 5 seconds with the hand test); see page 6.

4. Transfer the tenderloins to the grill, arranging them so that the thin end is angled away from the hottest part of the fire. Grill the tenderloins, uncovered, on high heat for 3 minutes, rolling them to sear on all sides. Move to medium heat and estimate the rest of the cooking time according to the thickness of the meat. Thin tenderloins (about 1½ inches in diameter) need another 10 to 12 minutes over medium heat; fat ones (about 2½ inches in diameter) require up to 25 minutes more. Continue rolling on all sides for even cooking. The pork is done when its internal temperature reaches 155° to 160°F.

5. Carve the pork into thin slices, garnish with avocado and tomato, and serve hot, passing the reserved *mojo*.

GRILLING TIP

Consider turning this tenderloin into a sandwich, the way *mojo*-flavored pork is often served in Florida. Pile the meat, a slice of ham, black beans, and sharp cheese on toasted Cuban bread or a crusty roll, then top it all with more *mojo*. Immensely sloppy and intensely good.

PORK TENDERLOIN FILLED WITH FIGS, BACON, AND CHARRED ONIONS

Double up a pair of tenderloins for this slightly fussy party dish. You butterfly each, sandwich a lusty filling between the two, secure them like a pretty present, and rub with a cracked pepper mixture. It's everybody's birthday at once. **SERVES 4 TO 6**

FILLING

1 medium-size onion, cut into 1/3-inch thick slices

About 8 metal or soaked bamboo skewers (optional)

Vegetable oil spray

4 ounces bacon, chopped

2 tablespoons unsalted butter

1 cup chopped dried figs (about 6 ounces)

2 tablespoons red wine vinegar or fig vinegar

3/4 cup coarse dried bread crumbs

About 1/2 cup chicken stock or water

Two 12- to 14-ounce pork tenderloins, butterflied and pounded to 1/2-inch thickness

Vegetable oil spray

DRY RUB

1 tablespoon cracked black peppercorns

1 teaspoon turbinado sugar or brown sugar

1 1/2 teaspoons kosher salt or coarse sea salt

BASTE

2 tablespoons unsalted butter

2 tablespoons chicken stock or water

2 teaspoons red wine vinegar or fig vinegar

1. Fire up the grill for a two-level fire capable of cooking at the same time on both high heat (1 to 2 seconds with the hand test) and medium heat (4 to 5 seconds with the hand test); see page 6.

2. First, make the filling. Run a skewer horizontally through each onion slice, if you wish, to help hold the rings together, then spray lightly with oil.

3. Grill the onion slices over medium heat until nearly tender with some charred edges, 8 to 10 minutes. Remove the onion slices and, when cool enough to handle, chop them coarsely. Warm a skillet over the grill's medium heat (or over a kitchen burner if you prefer). Fry the bacon in the skillet until brown and beginning to crisp. Remove the bacon with a slotted spoon and drain it on paper towels. To the drippings in the skillet, add the butter, chopped onion, and figs. Cook for several more minutes until the onion is soft, then stir in the vinegar, bread crumbs, and bacon. Remove from the heat and stir in enough stock to moisten the mixture. It should hold together easily and not be watery.

4. Trim the tenderloins to equal size. Spoon the filling evenly over one open tenderloin, almost to the edges. Top with the second open tenderloin. With several lengths of kitchen twine, tie the pork package up neatly. We go around the tenderloins lengthwise twice, and then turn and crisscross the string a half-dozen times around their girth. Spray all over with vegetable oil. The whole package should be about 2 inches thick throughout. Stir together the dry rub ingredients and rub it over all sides of the pork.

5. Combine the baste ingredients in a small saucepan and heat at the edge of the grill or over a kitchen burner until the butter melts. Set aside near the grill.

6. Transfer the stuffed tenderloin to the grill, arranging it first over high heat. Grill, uncovered, for about 3 minutes per side. Roll the pork over to medium heat and continue to grill for another 18 to 22 minutes. Roll over several times and brush lightly each time with the baste. The pork is ready when an instant-read thermometer inserted into the filling reaches 155° to 160°F. If, after 22 minutes, the pork is not getting close to 155°F, the meat may be thicker than optimum or the grill may be losing heat over time. Cover the grill, if needed, for a few more minutes of cooking until done.

7. Let the pork rest for 5 minutes, loosely tented with foil. Snip off the string. Cut into 1-inch-thick slices down through the filling and both layers of meat. Transfer carefully to plates so that the filling stays sandwiched between the layers of tenderloin.

DR PEPPER'S BABY BACK RIBS

Many backyard cooks roast pork ribs in a covered grill at a moderately low temperature for 3 hours or so. It's the exact same method you would use in an indoor oven for baking the ribs, and the meat tastes the same. We take a slightly different approach with baby backs, applying a dry rub first, wrapping the ribs in foil to keep the spices in place, and then baking them in a covered grill or oven for a couple of hours to tenderize the meat. After that, we remove the foil and finish the ribs on the direct heat of an open grill, basting with barbecue sauce and crusting the surface. **SERVES 4 OR MORE**

Three $1^3/_4$- to 2-pound slabs pork baby back ribs

DRY RUB

$1/_3$ cup smoked paprika

2 tablespoons smoked salt, preferably, or kosher or coarse sea salt

2 tablespoons turbinado sugar or 1 tablespoon packed light brown sugar

1 tablespoon chili powder

DR PEPPER BARBECUE SAUCE

$1/_4$ cup bacon drippings or other meat drippings, or vegetable oil

$1^1/_2$ cups chopped onion

2 to 4 fresh or pickled jalapeños or serrano chiles, seeded (if you wish) and chopped

One 12-ounce bottle or can Dr Pepper soda

1 cup ketchup

$3/_4$ cup Worcestershire sauce

$1/_4$ cup brewed black coffee

$1/_4$ cup cider vinegar

2 tablespoons molasses

2 tablespoons chili powder

2 tablespoons yellow mustard

1 to 2 teaspoons kosher or coarse sea salt

1. To strip off the thin membrane on the ribs' underside, make a cut or two into the membrane at one end of the rack, nudge the knife or your fingers under it, and then pull it off. (If you're a real fan of ribs, dedicate a pair of clean needle-nose pliers to this task and keep them in the kitchen or near the grill.) It should come off pretty much in one piece. Discard the membrane.

2. Plan on a total cooking time of at least 3 hours before you want to serve the ribs, though it is possible to do the initial long baking step a day ahead if you want. Preheat the oven or covered gas grill to 275°F. (If your grill is fueled with charcoal, use the oven for the first stage of baking the ribs, rather than try to keep the grill fire going for a lengthy period at a steady temperature.) Combine the dry rub ingredients in a small bowl. Set aside 2 tablespoons of the rub. Coat the ribs liberally on all sides with the remaining spice mixture.

3. Wrap the ribs tightly in two layers of foil, place on a baking sheet, and bake for 2 hours. The meat should begin to shrink away from the ends of the bones, exposing them a bit, and if you tug at a rib, it should pull apart with little resistance. Pour off and discard any accumulated grease and liquid.

4. Prepare the sauce while the ribs bake. Warm the drippings in a saucepan over medium heat. Stir in the onions and jalapeños and sauté until the onion is soft and translucent, about 5 minutes. Mix in the rest of the ingredients and bring to a simmer. Reduce the heat to low, cover, and cook for 30 minutes. Cool briefly. Puree the sauce in a blender, in batches if necessary. Reserve the warm sauce. (The sauce can be made up to several days in advance, covered, and refrigerated. Thin with a little water if it's too thick to brush easily.)

5. If you want to delay grilling the ribs for more than an hour, let them cool, opening the foil to speed the process. Rewrap the ribs in the foil and refrigerate them until about 30 minutes before you plan to grill.

6. When you are ready to proceed, fire up the grill, bringing the temperature to medium (4 to 5 seconds with the hand test).

7. Unwrap the ribs, discard the foil, and sprinkle the meaty side of the slabs equally with the reserved rub. Grill the ribs, uncovered, for a total of about 20 minutes. First grill on each side for about 7 minutes to crisp. Then baste the ribs generously with the sauce and cook for about 6 minutes more, letting each side face the fire briefly. The ribs are done when the surface is crusty in some spots and gooey with sauce in others. Serve the ribs hot, with more sauce and plenty of napkins.

bake, grill, and baste with a soft drink–enhanced sauce

SOUTH SEAS BABY BACKS

The flavor of coconuts works as well—if not better—in savory dishes as in desserts. In this case we use coconut milk as the base for a glaze flavored additionally with hoisin sauce and chili paste. **SERVES 4 OR MORE**

Three 1³/4- to 2-pound slabs pork baby back ribs

3 tablespoons rice vinegar

3 tablespoons Dijon mustard

2 teaspoons kosher or coarse sea salt

1 teaspoon Asian chili paste or chili-garlic paste or ¹/4 teaspoon cayenne pepper

GLAZE

One 14- to 15-ounce can unsweetened coconut milk (not cream of coconut)

3 tablespoons hoisin sauce

2 tablespoons honey or agave nectar

2 tablespoons Dijon mustard

1 teaspoon Chinese chili paste or chili-garlic paste or ¹/4 teaspoon cayenne pepper

1. To strip off the thin membrane on the ribs' underside, make a cut or two into the membrane at one end of the rack, nudge the knife or your fingers under it, and then pull it off. (If you're a real fan of ribs, dedicate a pair of clean needle-nose pliers to this task and keep them in the kitchen or near the grill.) It should come off pretty much in one piece. Discard the membrane.

2. Plan on a total cooking time of at least 3 hours before you want to serve the ribs, though it is possible to do the initial long baking step a day ahead if you want. Preheat the oven or covered gas grill to 275°F. (If your grill is fueled with charcoal, use the oven for the first stage of baking the ribs, rather than try to keep the grill fire going for a lengthy period at a steady temperature.) Whisk together the vinegar, mustard, salt, and chili paste in a small bowl. Rub the ribs liberally on all sides with the mixture.

3. Wrap the ribs tightly in two layers of foil, place on a baking sheet, and bake for 2 hours. The meat should start to shrink away from the ends of the bones, exposing them a bit, and if you tug at a rib, it should pull apart with little resistance. Pour off and discard any accumulated grease and liquid.

4. While the ribs bake, combine the glaze ingredients in a medium-size heavy saucepan, and bring to a boil over high heat. Reduce the heat and simmer the glaze for 20 to 25 minutes, until reduced to the consistency of thin syrup. Reserve the glaze at room temperature if you plan to grill the ribs within 1 hour; otherwise, cover and refrigerate it. (The glaze can be made several days in advance. Thin with a little water if it is too thick to brush easily.)

5. If you want to delay grilling the ribs for more than an hour, let them cool, opening the foil to speed the process. Rewrap the ribs in the foil and refrigerate them until about 30 minutes before you plan to grill.

6. When you are ready to proceed, fire up the grill, bringing the temperature to medium (4 to 5 seconds with the hand test).

7. Unwrap the ribs and discard the foil. Grill the ribs, uncovered, for a total of about 20 minutes. First grill on each side for about 7 minutes to crisp. Then baste the ribs generously with the glaze and cook for about 6 minutes more, letting each side face the fire briefly. The ribs are done when the surface is crusty in some spots and gooey with glaze in others. Serve the ribs hot.

POMEGRANATE LAMB CHOPS

For a change of pace and taste, few options satisfy as many people as lamb, and chops in particular are elegant and easy to prepare. Either loin or rib chops grill up great. Loin chops, looking like thick mini T-bones, have more meat, and rib chops appear even more dramatic, with their soaring bone and a succulent morsel or two of meat. You can trade out one for the other by comparing the grilling instructions in this and the next recipe. **SERVES 4**

Eight 1-inch-thick loin lamb chops (about 5 ounces each)

MARINADE

1 1/2 cups pomegranate juice

2 tablespoons extra-virgin olive oil

4 garlic cloves, minced

2 teaspoons dried rosemary, crushed

1/2 teaspoon kosher salt or coarse sea salt

Fresh rosemary sprigs, for garnish (optional)

1. Place the chops in a shallow nonreactive pan or zipper-top plastic bag.

2. Whisk together the marinade ingredients in a small bowl. Pour the marinade over the chops. Refrigerate for at least 2 hours and up to 4 hours, turning the meat at least once if it's not entirely submerged.

3. About 30 minutes before cooking, take the chops from the refrigerator and drain the marinade into a saucepan. Boil the marinade vigorously over high heat for several minutes.

4. Fire up the grill for a two-level fire capable of cooking at the same time on both high heat (1 to 2 seconds with the hand test) and medium heat (4 to 5 seconds with the hand test); see page 6.

5. Grill the chops, uncovered, over high heat for 1½ to 2 minutes per side. Move the chops to medium heat, turning them again, and continue grilling for about a minute per side for medium-rare. Rotate a half turn each time the chops are turned over for crisscross grill marks.

6. Serve the chops immediately, with spoonfuls of the reduced marinade sauce drizzled over the top. Garnish the plates with rosemary sprigs if you wish.

few options satisfy as many people as lamb, and chops in particular are elegant and easy to prepare

DEVILED LAMB RIB CHOPS

Seasoning grilled food with a paste—such as the mustard paste we use here—works faster than a marinade and imparts a greater punch of flavor. Here it also brings a hint of hellfire to the lamb. For a fancy-pants dinner, we ask our butcher to "french" the chops, which means that the long bones will be scraped clean. That technique loses some bone-gnawing meat and fat, though, so for casual eat-with-the-hands occasions, we keep the chops *au naturel*. Use whichever style suits you. **SERVES 4**

DEVILED MUSTARD PASTE

2 tablespoons spicy brown mustard

1 tablespoon yellow mustard

1 teaspoon cracked yellow mustard seeds

3/4 teaspoon cracked black peppercorns

1/2 teaspoon Tabasco or other hot pepper sauce

1/4 teaspoon kosher salt or coarse sea salt

Twelve 3/4- to -1-inch-thick lamb rib chops

Flaky sea salt (such as Maldon) or *fleur de sel*

1. At least 30 minutes before you plan to grill the chops, combine the paste ingredients in a small bowl. Smear it over the chops, including the rib bones. Let the chops sit, uncovered, at room temperature if you will be grilling shortly, or wrap and refrigerate for up to 4 hours.

2. Fire up the grill for a two-level fire capable of cooking at the same time on both high heat (1 to 2 seconds with the hand test) and medium heat (4 to 5 seconds with the hand test); see page 6.

3. Grill the chops, uncovered, over high heat for 1½ to 2 minutes per side. Move the chops to medium heat, rotating them a half turn for crisscross grill marks, and continue grilling for about 2 minutes per side for medium-rare doneness.

4. Arrange three chops on each plate, bones leaning against each other, scatter a few flakes of salt over the chops, and serve.

GRILLING TIP

Crack mustard seeds, peppercorns, or other whole spices by placing them in a small zipper-top plastic bag and then giving them a few whacks with a meat pounder.

CHICKEN, DUCK, AND QUAIL

BODACIOUS BARBECUED CHICKEN BREASTS

This is a fail-proof version of the all-American backyard classic, juicy chicken coated in sauce with a few charred and chewy edges. When it's grilled the traditional way, using bone-in skin-on chicken parts, it can be a challenge to cook it evenly all over and to avoid bad flare-ups from the skin and sauce. So we came up with this rendition made with boneless skinless breasts pounded to an even thickness for easy grilling. Whip up this special sauce or try one of the suggestions on page 128. **SERVES 4**

BARBECUE SAUCE

1 cup ketchup

1/4 cup molasses

2 tablespoons packed brown sugar

2 tablespoons butter

1 1/2 tablespoons Worcestershire sauce

2 teaspoons yellow mustard

1 teaspoon onion powder

1/2 teaspoon kosher salt or coarse sea salt

1/4 teaspoon freshly ground black pepper

1/4 teaspoon chili powder

1/2 cup water

3 to 4 tablespoons bourbon

4 large boneless, skinless chicken breast halves (6 to 7 ounces each), pounded to a thickness of 1/2 inch

1/2 cup Worcestershire sauce

2 teaspoons vegetable oil

1/2 teaspoon kosher salt or coarse sea salt

1. Combine the ketchup, molasses, brown sugar, butter, Worcestershire, mustard, onion powder, salt, pepper, chili powder, and water in a medium-size saucepan and bring to a boil. Reduce the heat to a bare simmer and cook for 5 to 10 minutes, until thickened lightly. Stir in the bourbon and simmer for another couple of minutes. Remove from the heat and set aside about half of the sauce to serve with the chicken at the table.

2. Place the chicken in a zipper-top plastic bag and pour the Worcestershire over it. Add the oil and salt, and seal the bag. Toss back and forth to coat the chicken evenly. Let sit at room temperature for 20 to 30 minutes.

3. Fire up the grill, bringing the temperature to medium (4 to 5 seconds with the hand test).

4. Drain the chicken, discarding the marinade, and blot any moisture on the surface with a paper towel.

5. Grill, uncovered, for 10 to 12 minutes total. Turn three times, rotating the breasts a half turn each time for crisscross grill marks. After each side of the chicken has faced the fire once, begin brushing the sauce over the breasts. The chicken is ready when it is white throughout but still juicy and the sauce is a bit chewy and caramelized in spots. If you wish, leave the chicken on the grill an extra minute or two to get a slightly crusty surface.

6. The breasts can be served whole or thickly sliced and mounded onto a platter. Pass the remaining sauce on the side.

While a tomato-based barbecue sauce is the most typical type for this dish, consider experimenting with other styles of barbecue sauce popular in various areas:

- Tangy yellow mustard sauce made with approximately equal amounts of mustard, distilled white vinegar, and butter, melted together.

- Even tangier vinegar sauce made with 1 cup cider vinegar or distilled white vinegar, 1 tablespoon sugar, 1 teaspoon salt, and 1/2 teaspoon freshly ground black pepper or crushed red pepper or both.

- White sauce, made with 1 cup mayonnaise, 1 to 2 tablespoons cider vinegar, 1 tablespoon coarsely ground black pepper, a few pinches of onion powder, and salt to taste.

a fail-proof version of the all-American backyard classic, juicy chicken coated in sauce with a few charred and chewy edges

CHICKEN BREASTS STUFFED WITH COUNTRY HAM

Cutting a pocket in a chicken breast and stuffing it with ham and herbs adds bold flavor from the inside out. Start with large breasts, and use a salty country ham sliced as thin as possible, or a similar quantity of prosciutto or speck, a German style of ham becoming more widely available. **SERVES 4**

> 4 large boneless, skinless chicken breast halves (6 to 7 ounces each), pounded to a thickness of 1/2 inch
>
> 5 teaspoons brown or Dijon mustard, plus more for serving
>
> Kosher salt or coarse sea salt
>
> 3 ounces aged country ham, prosciutto, or speck, sliced paper-thin, then finely chopped by hand
>
> 2 teaspoons minced fresh sage or 1 teaspoon crumbled dried sage
>
> 2 tablespoons unsalted butter, melted

1. Fire up the grill, bringing the temperature to medium (4 to 5 seconds with the hand test).

2. Slicing a pocket into each chicken breast is easiest to do when the chicken is very cold. Slice horizontally into a breast from one of its long sides. Use a small sharp knife, keeping the knife cut about 1 inch wide on the surface and sliding the blade back and forth inside the breast so that you form a space at least a couple of inches wide. Rub 1 teaspoon of the mustard inside each breast's pocket. Sprinkle inside and out with salt. Mix together the ham and sage and stuff an equal portion inside each breast.

3. Whisk the remaining 1 teaspoon mustard into the melted butter.

4. Grill the chicken, uncovered, for 10 to 12 minutes total. Turn three times, rotating the breasts a half turn each time for crisscross grill marks. After each side of the chicken has faced the fire once, brush the butter-mustard mixture lightly over the breasts, just dabbing a bit of it across each side when face up. The chicken is ready when it is white throughout but still juicy.

5. Let the chicken rest for several minutes, then cut each breast into individual slices and fan them on plates. Serve immediately, with additional dollops of mustard if you wish.

CHICKEN PAILLARDS WITH HOT GINGER SAUCE

Chicken breasts going to the grill always benefit from being pounded lightly to an even thickness, as we've done in the two previous recipes. In the case of paillards, we pound the poultry even thinner than usual, preferably placing the breasts between sheets of waxed paper or plastic wrap and striking them with a steady, moderate pressure rather than heavy blows. The broader surfaces give even more area to take on the flavors of a lively sauce. (We use smaller breasts for this technique because anything much larger gets rather unwieldy on the grill once it's pounded out.) Serve the paillards with tangy greens and white or brown rice to soak up the juices. SERVES 4

HOT GINGER SAUCE

2 tablespoons peanut oil

2 tablespoons minced or slivered fresh ginger

2 garlic cloves, minced

1/4 teaspoon crushed red pepper

1 cup chicken stock

1 teaspoon mirin (Japanese sweet rice wine) or 1/2 teaspoon sugar

4 small boneless, skinless chicken breast halves (about 4 ounces each), pounded to a thickness of 1/4 inch and ragged edges trimmed

Peanut oil

Kosher salt or coarse sea salt

1. Fire up the grill, bringing the temperature to medium (4 to 5 seconds with the hand test).

2. While the grill heats, prepare the sauce. Heat the oil in a small skillet until very hot, then add the ginger, garlic, and red pepper, and cook for 1 minute. Pour in the stock

and mirin, bring to a boil, and boil the sauce briefly, until reduced by half. Set aside about half of the sauce to serve with the chicken at the table.

3. Rub both sides of the paillards lightly with peanut oil and sprinkle lightly with salt on both sides.

4. Grill, uncovered, for 7 to 8 minutes total. Turn three times, rotating the paillards a half turn each time for crisscross grill marks. After each side of the chicken has faced the fire once, begin brushing the sauce over the paillards. The chicken is ready when white throughout but still juicy.

5. Serve the paillards immediately, sliced and topped with the remaining sauce.

the broader surfaces give even more area to take on the flavors of a lively sauce

55

ORANGE-CHIPOTLE CHICKEN BREASTS

After you've mastered the first recipe in the chapter, you may want to advance to this one. Bone-in, skin-on chicken parts—such as these breasts—come off a grill with more flavor and juicy zest than their naked, boneless counterparts. The skin keeps the meat from drying out and its fat bastes the chicken naturally as it cooks. You can take the skin off before eating the chicken if you're concerned about calories and fat, but if we happen to be around, please pass it to us. **SERVES 4**

ORANGE-CHIPOTLE SAUCE

1/2 cup fresh orange juice (zest from the fruit grated and reserved for the chicken)

1/4 cup plus 2 tablespoons chicken stock

1/4 cup plus 1 tablespoon ketchup

1 to 2 canned chipotle chiles in adobo sauce, minced, plus 2 teaspoons adobo sauce

1/4 cup orange marmalade

1 tablespoon fresh lime juice

1 tablespoon unsalted butter

1/4 teaspoon kosher salt or coarse sea salt, or more to taste

Grated zest from the oranges used for the sauce

2 teaspoons vegetable oil

1 teaspoon kosher salt or coarse sea salt, or more to taste

4 large bone-in, skin-on chicken breast halves (8 to 10 ounces each)

1. Stir together the sauce ingredients in a small saucepan. Bring to a boil over medium heat, then reduce to a bare simmer and cook for about 5 minutes. Let the sauce cool to room temperature.

2. About 30 minutes before you plan to grill the chicken breasts, stir together the reserved orange zest, oil, and salt. Loosen the skin on the breasts. Rub the mixture lightly onto the breasts, over and under the skin, being careful to avoid tearing it or pulling it loose. Cover the breasts and let sit at room temperature for 20 to 30 minutes.

3. Fire up the grill, bringing the temperature to medium (4 to 5 seconds with the hand test).

4. Blot any moisture on the surface of the chicken with a paper towel. Transfer the chicken to the grill, skin side down. Grill, uncovered, for 30 to 35 minutes total, turning at least four times. (The chicken skin should face the grill enough to render fat and cook gradually without burning.) If one edge of the breasts is much thinner than the other, arrange the chicken so that the thinner edges are toward the outer, cooler edge of the fire. Watch for flare-ups, shifting the breasts away from the flame as necessary. After you have turned the chicken twice, brush thickly with the sauce. If any of the pieces start to burn—rather than just get a few chewy, charred edges—move them away from direct flames as much as possible while they finish cooking. End with the chicken skin side down to give it a final crisping. When done, the chicken should be white throughout but still juicy, and register 170°F on an instant-read thermometer. Serve immediately.

> the skin keeps the meat from drying
> out and its fat bastes the chicken
> naturally as it cooks

56

AFRICAN CHICKEN

These bone-in breasts and thighs boast a powerful kick from chile, originally a small African chile named piri piri. Portuguese settlers in the country's African colonies brought the chile home and then sent it around the world to other imperial outposts. Chicken flavored with the pod became especially popular in Macau, the former Portuguese colony next door to Hong Kong. To this day, cooks there call this dish "African Chicken." It tastes best when the chicken has had the chance to spend at least a few hours in the marinade, so plan accordingly. Serve with more hot sauce tableside, if you like. **SERVES 4**

AFRICAN MARINADE AND SAUCE

3/4 cup top-quality extra-virgin olive oil

1/4 cup bottled piri piri hot sauce or other hot pepper sauce

1/4 cup fresh lemon juice

2 plump shallots, minced

4 medium-size bone-in, skin-on chicken breast halves (6 to 7 ounces each)

4 medium-size bone-in, skin-on chicken leg-thigh sections (8 to 9 ounces each)

Kosher salt or coarse sea salt

1. Stir together the marinade ingredients in a small bowl and reserve one-third of it for a table sauce.

2. Season the chicken parts generously with salt, rubbing some of it under the skin, but being careful to avoid tearing the skin. Place the chicken in a zipper-top plastic bag and pour the marinade over it. Toss back and forth to coat the chicken evenly. Refrigerate for at least 3 hours and up to 12 hours. Drain the chicken and blot any moisture on the surface with a paper towel. Let sit at room temperature for 20 to 30 minutes.

3. Fire up the grill, bringing the temperature to medium (4 to 5 seconds with the hand test).

4. Transfer the chicken to the grill, skin side down. Grill, uncovered, for 30 to 35 minutes total, turning at least four times. (The chicken skin should face the grill enough to render fat and cook gradually without burning.) If one edge of the breasts is much thinner than the other, arrange the chicken so that the thinner edges are toward the outer, cooler edge of the fire. Watch for flare-ups, shifting the chicken away from the flames as necessary. End with the chicken skin side down to give it a final crisping. The chicken is done when white throughout but still juicy, and it registers 170°F on an instant-read thermometer. Breasts and thighs should be done at about the same time, but check the temperature in at least one breast and one thigh before removing.

5. Serve immediately, passing the reserved sauce at the table, for those who wish.

CHICKEN THIGHS WITH LOADS OF LEMON AND GARLIC

The deeper-flavored dark meat of chicken thighs and legs benefits from grilling over a two-level fire rather than steady medium heat. Start with a hot fire to sear the meat and then finish the cooking over medium-low heat. We bathe these thighs in a refreshing marinade based on lemon and garlic. **SERVES 4**

LEMON AND GARLIC MARINADE

2 tablespoons extra-virgin olive oil

1 heaping tablespoon minced garlic

Grated zest and juice of 1 large lemon

1 teaspoon kosher salt or coarse sea salt

1/4 teaspoon freshly ground black pepper

8 large bone-in, skin-on chicken thighs (about 7 ounces each)

1. At least 2 hours and up to 24 hours before you plan to grill, prepare the marinade. Combine the oil, garlic, and lemon zest in a small skillet and warm over medium-low heat for several minutes, until the garlic begins to color. Remove from the heat and let cool. Stir in the lemon juice, salt, and pepper. The mixture will be soupy.

2. Loosen the skin on the thighs. Coat the thighs thoroughly with the marinade, rubbing it over and under the skin, working it as far as possible under the skin without tearing it. Place the chicken in a zipper-top plastic bag with any remaining marinade, seal the bag, and refrigerate.

3. Remove the chicken from the refrigerator, discarding the marinade, and let it sit, uncovered, at room temperature for 20 to 30 minutes.

4. Fire up the grill for a two-level fire capable of cooking at the same time on both high heat (1 to 2 seconds with the hand test) and medium-low heat (5 to 6 seconds with the hand test); see page 6.

5. Blot any liquid on the surface of the chicken with a paper towel. Grill, uncovered, over high heat for 3 to 4 minutes, turning to sear both sides. Move the chicken to medium-low heat and continue grilling for another 12 to 15 minutes, turning every 3 minutes or so. Watch for flare-ups, shifting the thighs away from the flames if necessary. The thighs are done when the skin is brown and crisp and the juices run clear. The temperature should register 170°F on an instant-read thermometer. Serve immediately.

the deeper-flavored dark meat of chicken thighs and legs benefits from grilling over a two-level fire

CHICKEN UNDER A BRICK

Italians call this popular dish *pollo al mattone*, which translates literally as "chicken under a heavy tile." Use a *mattone* if you have one, or a pizza stone, a foil-wrapped brick or two, a cast-iron skillet, or any other nonflammable object that will force a chicken half to lie flat on the grill. The weight also deflects and absorbs some of the heat, allowing the chicken to cook through without scorching. Buy a whole chicken and ask the butcher to remove the backbone and butterfly the bird, or do the job yourself, as we explain below.

SERVES 2 TO 4

One 3- to 3 1/2-pound chicken

1 tablespoon minced fresh rosemary

1 1/2 teaspoons kosher salt or coarse sea salt

1 teaspoon coarsely ground black pepper

1 large lemon, sliced lengthwise into 4 wedges, for serving

1. Your butcher can prepare the chicken for you, but the process is not hard if you have a good pair of kitchen scissors. First, cut the chicken in half down the back, cutting along each side of the backbone and discarding it. Then cut off the wing tips, the outermost wing joints. With the chicken skin side up, use your hands to press down on the breast area with medium pressure to crack the breastbone and flatten the chicken for even cooking. Use a mallet to pound the chicken lightly and evenly, making it a uniform 1 to 1 1/2 inches in thickness.

2. Combine the rosemary, salt, and pepper in a small bowl. Rub the chicken with the mixture inside and out, working it as far as possible under the skin without tearing it. Let the chicken sit, covered, at room temperature for 20 to 30 minutes.

3. Fire up the grill, bringing the temperature to medium (4 to 5 seconds with the hand test).

4. Transfer the chicken to the grate, skin side down, stretching it out fully. Arrange its neck and tail ends in the direction of the cooking grate bars to create more attractive vertical stripes from the grill rather than horizontal. Cover with a pizza stone or other weight of several pounds. Grill the chicken, uncovered, for a total of 35 to 45 minutes. Turn the chicken once, after about 20 minutes, replacing the stone to continue cooking. In the last 5 minutes or so of cooking, use tongs to nudge the lemon quarters around the edges of the chicken so that they can char lightly. The chicken is done when it has crispy, golden-brown skin and registers 170° to 175°F on an instant-read thermometer inserted into the thickest portion of a thigh.

5. To serve, carve through or along the breastbone, then cut into breast and leg portions as you wish. Serve each portion with 1 or more lemon quarters.

Italians call this popular dish **pollo al mattone,** *which translates as* **"chicken under a heavy tile"**

GRILLED DUCK BREASTS WITH ARMAGNAC AND LAVENDER HONEY GLAZE

Duck breasts can be grilled to crispy perfection with a little special treatment. Variations of this recipe have been especially popular with culinary groups that we have taken to France's duck and goose capital, the Dordogne, for many years. For us personally, it's a no-brainer to rank this recipe as one of our top 100 grill dishes. **SERVES 6**

6 small boneless, skin-on duck breast halves (about 6 ounces each)

1 teaspoon kosher salt or coarse sea salt

1 tablespoon dried *herbes de Provence*

ARMAGNAC AND HONEY GLAZE

1 tablespoon unsalted butter or rendered duck fat

1/3 cup minced shallots

1/2 teaspoon dried *herbes de Provence*

1/2 cup Armagnac or brandy

3/4 cup duck or chicken stock

1/4 cup lavender honey, or other honey with a couple of pinches of dried culinary lavender buds added

Kosher salt or coarse sea salt

1. At least 1 hour and up to 24 hours before you plan to grill, prepare the duck breasts. If the skin is any thicker than 1/4 inch, trim it to that thickness with a sharp knife, shearing off portions as needed. Also slice off any portions of skin or fat that hang beyond the edges of the meat. (Save the skin and fat trimmings.) Make shallow criss-cross cuts down through the remaining skin on the breasts. Make the cuts about 1/2 inch apart, and cut through the skin but not into the flesh. This promotes gradual and easy rendering of fat, and offers more surfaces for the seasonings to flavor.

2. Combine the salt and *herbes de Provence* in a small bowl. Massage the herb mixture into the duck breasts, rubbing it over and under the skin. Let sit, uncovered, at room temperature while you prepare the glaze.

3. For the glaze, place the butter and reserved duck trimmings in a small saucepan. Over medium-low heat, render the fat from the duck trimmings until you have about 3 tablespoons. (The few bits of crispy duck skin are the cook's treat.) Should you not have enough rendered fat, add butter to make 3 tablespoons of drippings. Add the shallots to the fat and cook for 1 to 2 minutes, until soft. Add the *herbes de Provence*, stir in the Armagnac, and cook down by half over medium heat. Add the stock and honey and cook, stirring, until the honey melts into the glaze. Season with salt to taste. Reserve half of the glaze for serving.

4. Fire up the grill, bringing the temperature to medium (4 to 5 seconds with the hand test). Have enough grate space available so that you will be able to move the breasts around as needed when flare-ups occur.

5. On the grill or stovetop, heat a cast-iron or other heavy skillet over medium heat. When warm, add the duck breasts, skin side down, and cook until the skin has rendered most of its remaining fat and turned golden.

6. Remove the duck breasts to a plate and brush on all sides with half of the glaze. Transfer the duck breasts to the grill, skin side up, and grill, uncovered, for about 4 minutes, rotating a half turn after about 2 minutes for crisscross grill marks. Turn skin side down and cook for about 4 minutes more, rotating a half turn again halfway through cooking. Grill until the skin is deep golden brown and crisp and the meat is medium-rare. Watch for flare-ups, moving the breasts away from the flames as necessary. Turn the breasts over and grill skin side up for an additional 2 to 3 minutes for medium-rare.

7. Slice the duck thinly, so that each piece has a bit of the crisp skin, and fan the slices on plates. Drizzle portions with the remaining glaze. Serve hot.

DUCK JAMBALAYA

Grilling the main cuts of poultry and meat in a jambalaya gives the dish a tasty outdoor flavor. The grilling technique is also ideal for poultry, meat, and seafood that get combined with rice or pastas, from paella to ravioli to pot stickers. Here the duck is cooked a bit differently, and a little more simply, than in the previous recipe. You don't need it to look especially lovely because the meat will be cut up and mixed in with the rice. **SERVES 4**

FOR THE GRILL

2 small boneless, skin-on duck breast halves (about 6 ounces each)

Kosher salt or coarse sea salt

Freshly ground black pepper

4 ounces andouille or other smoked pork sausage links, such as kielbasa

FOR THE POT

2 tablespoons vegetable oil

1 medium-size onion, chopped

2 ounces tasso (Cajun seasoned ham), country ham, or other smoky ham, minced

3/4 cup minced celery

1 large green bell pepper, seeded and chopped

2 plump garlic cloves, minced

1 bay leaf

1 1/2 teaspoons kosher salt or coarse sea salt

3/4 teaspoon dried crumbled thyme

1 cup uncooked long-grain white rice

1 1/2 cups chicken stock

1/4 teaspoon Tabasco or other Louisiana hot pepper sauce, or more to taste

Fresh thyme sprigs, for garnish (optional)

1. If the duck breast skin is any thicker than 1/4 inch, trim it to that thickness with a sharp knife, shearing off portions as needed. Also slice off any portions of skin or fat that hang beyond the edges of the meat. Make shallow crisscross cuts down through the remaining skin on the breasts. Make the cuts about 1/2 inch apart, and cut through the skin but not into the flesh. This will help the seasonings flavor the duck more fully and promotes gradual and easy rendering of fat during cooking. Rub salt and pepper over the breasts and let them and the andouille sit, uncovered, at room temperature while you prepare the grill.

2. Fire up the grill, bringing the temperature to medium (4 to 5 seconds with the hand test). You will need enough grate space available so that you can move the duck breasts around as needed when flare-ups occur. If you would like to cook the rice over the grill fire, instead of on a side burner or stovetop, you'll need a skillet with a heatproof handle and the capability for high heat (1 to 2 seconds with the hand test) and medium-low heat (5 to 6 seconds) as well.

3. Begin the rice. Warm the oil in a heavy 8- to 10-inch skillet over high heat. Mix in the onion and tasso, and sauté until the onion is browned, about 8 minutes. Add the celery, bell pepper, and garlic, reduce the heat to medium, and continue cooking until the vegetables are softened, about 5 minutes. Stir in the bay leaf, salt, and thyme, followed by the rice, and cook for about 3 minutes longer, until the rice grains are translucent. Pour in the stock and Tabasco. Bring just to a boil, then reduce the heat to medium-low. Cover and cook until the rice is tender and the liquid is absorbed, 18 to 20 minutes, stirring up from the bottom once about halfway through the cooking time.

4. While the rice cooks, grill the duck breasts and andouille. Transfer the breasts to the grill skin side down. Grill, uncovered, for 4 to 6 minutes, watching carefully and moving the duck around as needed to minimize flare-ups. Cook until the skin is deep golden brown and crisp. Turn the breasts skin side up and grill for another 3 to 4 minutes for medium, then slice into cubes, ensuring that most pieces have some of the crisp skin. Simultaneously, grill the andouille, rolling it around on all sides, until nicely brown and a bit crisp, 6 to 10 minutes, depending on size. Slice the andouille into thin half-moons.

5. Remove the rice from the heat when done, and let it sit, covered, for 10 minutes. Remove the bay leaf from the rice. Stir the duck and andouille and any accumulated juices into the rice. Spoon the jambalaya into a large bowl or onto plates. Garnish with thyme sprigs, if you wish, and serve.

QUAIL WITH RED-EYE RUB

The coffee-based rub on these quail halves wake up both the bird and the eater. Most of your friends probably think of quail as exotic, but the birds are easy to grill. Opt for semi-boneless quail, if you can. If all you can find are whole quail, it's simple to cut them into halves through their backbone and breastbone with kitchen scissors. **SERVES 4**

RED-EYE RUB

2 tablespoons coarse-ground coffee beans

1 tablespoon coarsely ground black pepper

1 heaping teaspoon kosher salt or coarse sea salt

8 quail, preferably semi-boneless, halved

1. At least 2 hours and up to 8 hours before you plan to grill, Combine the rub ingredients in a small bowl. Loosen the quail skin gently because it is much more fragile than that of a chicken or duck. Coat the quail with the rub, massaging it over and under the skin without tearing it. Place the quail in a large zipper-top plastic bag and refrigerate.

2. Fire up the grill, bringing the temperature to medium (4 to 5 seconds with the hand test).

3. Remove the quail from the refrigerator and let sit, covered, at room temperature for about 20 minutes.

4. Grill the quail, uncovered, for 4 to 6 minutes per side, rotating a half turn about halfway through the grilling on each side for crisscross grill marks. The quail are ready when the meat has turned opaque and the skin is brown and crisp. Expect the cooked quail to remain a little pinker than chicken. Serve the quail hot and feel free to pick it up with your fingers.

GRILLING AND THE MODEL T

People have cooked with charcoal for centuries, but the familiar briquettes of today are as new as the automobile age. In the past, people made charcoal by piling logs into a pyramid, covering the mound with earth to restrict air circulation, and burning the wood down to carbon. The process resulted in irregular lumps or chunks of high-heat fuel, useful for broiling or roasting food in an outside fire pit or an indoor wood stove. This style of charcoal still exists—and works great for grilling—but the briquette replaced it as the most popular cooking fuel thanks to Henry Ford's Model T.

Ford used a number of wood appointments in his early cars, parts cut to order at a mill he operated in the northern forests of Michigan. A man who hated waste as much as he loved profits, Ford became increasingly bothered by the mushrooming stacks of wood scraps at his plant. The pieces were too small to make regular charcoal, but he realized that he could still convert them to carbon, grind the coals into a powder, add a binding agent, and compress the granulated mixture into pillow-shaped briquettes.

Ford got his friend Thomas Edison to design a production facility, which went into full operation in 1921, a few decades ahead of its time. The auto magnate initially envisioned his little packets of firepower as an industrial fuel, to be sold directly to businesses. He later marketed the charcoal to the public through Ford dealerships, but he died too soon to see how and why backyard cooks would turn his product into an industry of its own. Compact, long-burning, and uniform in heat, briquettes were destined for the grill, but they arrived there with the speed of a Model T.

SPIT-ROASTED POULTRY AND MEAT

HERB-ROASTED ROTISSERIE CHICKEN

This was a shoo-in among our 100 favorites for this book. Nothing rivals spit-roasting in front of the fire as a way to cook a whole chicken—producing lusciously juicy, golden-crisp birds—but few grill manufacturers provide adequate instructions on how to do it well. That's also true of directions that come with rotisseries designed to cook above the fire, such as optional attachments for charcoal grills and pared-down or older gas models.

Here's our blueprint for success with both kinds of rotisseries. The directions are detailed because the process is completely new to many people. By the second time, you'll probably only glance at the instructions, and by the third time, we'll wager that you'll be flying solo. To serve more than four people, simply get other chickens close to the same size and cook multiple birds simultaneously.

SERVES 2 TO 4

> One 3$1/4$- to 3$1/2$-pound chicken
>
> Butter, extra-virgin olive oil, rendered goose or duck fat, or other flavorful fat (optional)
>
> Kosher salt or coarse sea salt
>
> Freshly ground black pepper
>
> Freshly minced herbs and sprigs, such as tarragon, rosemary, basil, or thyme

1. At least 1 hour and up to 24 hours ahead of when you plan to roast, season the chicken. If your rotisserie cooks in front of the flame rather than above it, and you want to use the fat for extra flavor, rub it on the chicken at the same time. Don't use the fat if you're cooking above the flame because much of it drips away and will increase flare-ups. Loosen the skin all over, gently nudging your fingers down under it, including the skin on the drumsticks. Rub the outside of the chicken generously with the

butter, salt, pepper, and minced herbs under and over the skin, being careful to avoid tearing the skin.

2. After rubbing, place a few herb sprigs into the chicken's body cavity. Place the chicken in a large zipper-top plastic bag, seal, and refrigerate for at least 30 minutes and up to 24 hours. Let sit at room temperature for about 20 minutes before proceeding.

3. Fire up the rotisserie, removing the spit first if it's in place, and heat the grill with the lid closed. Use the set rotisserie temperature, if your grill functions that way, or bring the heat to medium (4 to 5 seconds with the hand test).

4. Truss the chicken, which ensures even cooking and keeps the bird from flopping around on the spit. Cut a 4-foot length of kitchen twine. Set the chicken breast side up on a work surface. Starting in the middle of your piece of string, wrap it around the ends of both legs, then crisscross the string back and forth around the chicken up to the neck end. Pay special attention to the wing areas, since you want to have the wings flush against the chicken's body. Tie the string ends together when you have wrapped the rest snugly around the bird.

5. Slide one of the prongs onto the far end of the spit, facing toward the center. Next slide on the chicken, running the spit through the cavity, with the legs first. Secure the legs to the prong. Slide on the second prong and attach it to the chicken's neck end. (If you are adding a second chicken, or more, you will need a center prong piece that juts in both directions for each additional bird.)

6. Reposition the chicken in the center of the spit and tighten the bolts on the prongs. If your rotisserie has a counterweight that fits on the spit or its handle, secure it in place. Attach the spit to the motor and turn on the power. Close the grill cover unless the manufacturer's instructions say otherwise.

7. Cook until an instant-read thermometer stuck in the thickest part of a thigh reads 170° to 175°F, 70 to 90 minutes, depending on the type of rotisserie. Don't open the grill too often or you will increase the cooking time substantially.

8. With heatproof mitts, remove the spit from the grill. Unscrew the counterweight and bolts, and slide the chicken and prongs off. Set the chicken on a large cutting board. Pull off the prongs and snip off the twine. Tent the chicken loosely with foil. Let it sit for about 10 minutes, so the juices can settle, then carve and serve.

ST. TROPEZ MARKET CHICKENS WITH DRESSING

You might not expect it, but one of the earthiest and friendliest outdoor markets in France is in the upscale resort town of St. Tropez. Always one and sometimes several vendors set up big rotisserie cookers in the Saturday market, selling spit-roasted chickens bursting with sunny flavors like you'll find in these birds. The dressing we use here is awkward to make in a small quantity, so we cook two chickens to share the bounty. **SERVES 4 TO 6**

1/3 cup minced pitted French black or green olives, or a combination

2 tablespoons top-quality extra-virgin olive oil

2 teaspoons kosher salt or coarse sea salt

Two 3- to 3¹/4-pound chickens

DRESSING

12 ounces white country bread, torn into bite-size pieces (about 2¹/2 cups)

1/4 cup top-quality extra-virgin olive oil

1¹/2 cups chopped onion

1 cup chopped fennel (1 small bulb)

1 garlic clove, minced

2¹/2 tablespoons minced fresh thyme, sage, or rosemary, or a combination, *or* 1¹/4 teaspoons dried thyme, sage, or rosemary, or a combination

2 teaspoons minced fresh lemon zest

2 teaspoons fennel seeds, crushed

1/2 teaspoon crushed red pepper

2 to 3 cups roughly chopped chard leaves

1/2 to 1¹/2 cups chicken stock, as needed

Kosher salt or coarse sea salt (optional)

1. At least 1 hour and up to 24 hours before you plan to cook the chickens, combine the olives, oil, and salt in a small bowl. Loosen the skin all over, gently nudging your fingers down under it, including the skin on the drumsticks. Rub the mixture over the outside of the chickens, both over and under the skin, being careful to avoid tearing the skin. Place each chicken in a large zipper-top plastic bag, seal, and refrigerate. Remove them from the refrigerator and let sit at room temperature for about 20 minutes before stuffing them.

2. To make the dressing, first preheat the oven to 325°F. Toast the bread pieces on a baking sheet for about 25 minutes, stirring once or twice, until lightly brown and crisp. Dump them into a large bowl. (Leave the oven on if you're going to cook the chickens immediately.) Meanwhile, warm the oil in a large skillet over medium heat, and stir in the onion, fennel, garlic, herbs, lemon zest, fennel seeds, and red pepper. Cook until the onion and fennel are soft and browned in spots, about 15 minutes. Scrape up from the bottom occasionally to get all the bits that stick to the bottom of the skillet. Arrange the chard over the onion-fennel mixture. Cover, reduce the heat to low, and cook for 5 more minutes, until the chard has wilted just enough to look sorry and limp. Scrape the skillet mixture into the bowl with the toasted bread pieces. Combine the dressing with a sturdy spoon. Stir in enough stock to make the dressing moist, add salt if you wish, and then set aside to cool to room temperature. (The dressing can be made up to 24 hours ahead and refrigerated, covered. Bring to room temperature before proceeding.)

3. Fire up the rotisserie, removing the spit first if it's in place, and heat the grill with the lid closed. Use the set rotisserie temperature, if your grill functions that way, or bring the heat to medium (4 to 5 seconds with the hand test).

4. Spoon some of the dressing loosely into the cavity of each chicken; set aside the remainder. To truss each chicken, cut a 4-foot length of kitchen twine. Set the chicken breast side up on a work surface. Starting in the middle of your piece of string, wrap it around the ends of both legs, then crisscross the string back and forth around the chicken up to the neck end. Pay special attention to the wing areas, since you want to have the wings flush against the chicken's body. Tie the string ends together when you have wrapped the rest snugly around the bird.

5. Slide one of the prongs onto the far end of the spit, facing toward the center. Next slide on the first chicken, running the spit through the cavity, with the legs first.

Secure the legs to the prong. Slide on a center prong piece that juts in both directions, secure it to the chicken's neck end, and then slide on the second bird, securing the legs to the other end of the center prong piece. Finally, slide on the last prong and attach it to the second chicken's neck end.

6. Reposition the chickens in the center of the spit and tighten the bolts on the prongs. If your rotisserie has a counterweight that fits on the spit or its handle, secure it in place. Attach the spit to the motor and turn on the power. Close the grill cover unless the manufacturer's instructions say otherwise.

7. Cook until an instant-read thermometer stuck in the thickest part of a thigh reads 170° to 175°F, 70 to 90 minutes, depending on the type of rotisserie. Don't open the grill too often or you will increase the cooking time substantially.

8. While the chickens are cooking, add enough stock to the remaining dressing to saturate it, but don't make it soupy. Spoon this dressing into a greased shallow baking dish, cover it, and bake for 20 minutes at 325°F. Uncover and continue baking until crusty and golden, 15 to 20 minutes more.

9. When the chickens are done, remove the spit from the grill with heatproof mitts. Unscrew the counterweight and bolts, and slide the chickens and prongs off. Set the chickens on a large cutting board. Pull off the prongs and snip off the twine. Tent the chickens loosely with foil. Let them sit for about 10 minutes, so the juices can settle. Spoon the dressing out of the cavities. Slice the chickens and serve, with both dressings on the side.

GRILLING TIP

Every local open-air market in France includes at least one rotisserie chicken vendor cooking fare on site. Do as they do, arranging chunks of potatoes, carrots, onions, parsnips, and other roasting vegetables under the chicken so that they catch the scrumptious drippings. Cut the vegetables into 1-inch-size pieces, put them in a foil-lined pan, stir once or twice as they cook, and they'll be done at the same time as the bird.

DONE TO A TURN

When Americans cooked with a wood fire in kitchen hearths—a practice that lasted well into the nineteenth century—they often spit-roasted poultry and meat on a rotisserie positioned at the front of the fireplace and the flame. The method yields better results than modern oven roasting, basting foods in their natural fats while crisping the surface and retaining internal succulence. The live fire and revolving spit produce a dinner that's literally "done to a turn."

Now rotisserie roasting is enjoying a major resurgence. An increasing number of grills, particularly new gas models, feature a motorized spit placed in front of the cooking fire rather than above it. Among all the frills offered with grills today, this is the one that excites us the most. For whole birds and cuts of meat too large to grill over a direct flame, it provides a perfect alternative to grilling, giving results as similar as possible. Take a turn at it and you'll never go back.

BUTTERY HERITAGE TURKEY

A growing number of tradition-oriented American farms are raising heritage turkeys such as Bourbon Reds and Narragansetts. Prized for their rich flavor and bright plumage, they are the ancestors of the broad-breasted industrial breed of birds most common today. You won't find these turkeys in most supermarkets, but some farmers' market vendors raise them, and specialty food stores and a variety of websites sell them. Even though they cost more than the mass-market Thanksgiving birds, they give you a great new reason to rejoice. **SERVES 6 TO 8**

One 9- to 10-pound heritage turkey

2 to 3 tablespoons kosher salt or coarse sea salt

1/4 to 1/3 cup dried porcini or other wild mushrooms

6 tablespoons (3/4 stick) unsalted butter

About 1 cup chicken or turkey stock, if needed

1. Season the turkey with the salt up to 24 hours before you plan to roast it. Rehydrate the dried mushrooms in warm water to cover for about 20 minutes. Drain and mince. Melt the butter in a skillet over medium heat and sauté the mushrooms until well softened, about 5 minutes.

2. Slip your fingers under the turkey's skin and loosen it, being careful not to tear it. Rub the turkey generously inside and out with the salt and seasoned butter, especially under the breast skin. If your rotisserie cooks above the flame rather than in front of it, reduce the amount of butter (to minimize flare-ups) and rub it only under the turkey breast.

3. Truss the turkey. Cut a 10-foot length of kitchen twine. Set the turkey breast side up on a work surface. Starting in the middle of your piece of string, wrap it around the ends of both legs, then crisscross the string back and forth around the turkey up to the neck end. Pay special attention to the wing areas, since you want to have the wings flush against the turkey's body. Tie the string ends together when you have

wrapped the rest snugly around the bird. Let the turkey sit at room temperature for about 45 minutes.

4. Fire up the rotisserie, removing the spit first if it's in place, and heat the grill with the lid closed. Use the set rotisserie temperature, if your grill functions that way, or bring the heat to medium (4 to 5 seconds with the hand test).

5. Slide one of the prongs onto the far end of the spit, facing toward the center. Next slide on the turkey, running the spit through the cavity, with the neck end first. Secure the neck end to the prong, trying to get the prongs lodged centrally to help balance the bird's weight. Then slide on the second end prong and attach it to the turkey's legs.

6. Reposition the turkey in the center of the spit and tighten the bolts on the prongs. If your rotisserie has a counterweight that fits on the spit or its handle, secure it in place, generally angled outward from the backside of the turkey. Attach the spit to the motor and turn on the power. Place a drip pan under the bird to catch the drippings, unless your rotisserie sits directly over the fire and the pan would block the heat. Close the grill cover unless the manufacturer's instructions say otherwise.

7. Cook until an instant-read thermometer stuck in the thickest part of a thigh reads 175°F, 18 to 20 minutes per pound, or about 3 hours. Baste the turkey three or four times at 45-minute intervals with pan drippings if you have them or, if not, with chicken or turkey stock. Don't baste during the last 30 minutes of cooking, though, so the skin has a chance to crisp. Avoid opening the grill too many other times or you will increase the cooking time substantially.

8. When done, turn off the heat and the rotisserie motor. Let the turkey sit on the spit with the grill cover closed for 10 to 15 minutes. With heatproof mitts, remove the spit from the grill. Unscrew the counterweight and bolts, and slide the turkey and prongs off. Set the turkey on a large cutting board. Pull off the prongs and snip off the twine. Tent the turkey loosely with foil. Let sit for about 10 minutes more, so the juices can settle again, then carve and serve.

SPIT-ROASTED TURKEY BREAST

A whole turkey, cooked to a turn, is the ultimate in Thanksgiving grandeur, but it's not exactly casual party food. A turkey breast offers equally fine eating with a much smaller investment in time and logistics, making it a better option for many occasions. This basic preparation works great with any of the seasoning pastes described in the Grilling Tip on page 157. **SERVES 8 OR MORE**

One 4$\frac{1}{2}$- to 5$\frac{1}{2}$-pound bone-in, skin-on turkey breast

Kosher salt or coarse sea salt and freshly ground black pepper, or a favorite dry rub

Butter, extra-virgin olive oil, rendered goose or duck fat, or other flavorful fat (optional)

Fresh herb sprigs (optional)

1. At least 1 hour and up to 24 hours ahead of when you plan to roast the turkey breast, rub it with salt and pepper to taste. If your rotisserie cooks in front of the flame rather than above it, and you want to use the fat for extra flavor, rub it on the turkey breast at the same time. Don't use the fat if you're cooking above the flame because much of it will drip away and increase flare-ups. Loosen the skin all over, gently nudging your fingers down under it. Rub the turkey breast generously with the flavorings and optional herbs under and over the skin, being careful to avoid tearing the skin.

2. Place the turkey breast in a large zipper-top plastic bag, seal, and refrigerate until shortly before you plan to cook. Then let sit at room temperature for about 20 minutes before proceeding.

3. Fire up the rotisserie, removing the spit first if it's in place, and heat the grill with the lid closed. Use the set rotisserie temperature, if your grill functions that way, or bring the heat to medium (4 to 5 seconds with the hand test).

4. Slide one of the prongs onto the far end of the spit, facing toward the center. Next slide on the turkey breast, with what would have been its head end first. In order to distribute the weight evenly, run the spit halfway between the wings, but about 1 inch closer to the front of the breast than the back. If your spit end isn't fairly sharp,

you may need to poke a hole down through the breast with an ice pick, a pair of kitchen scissors, or a sharp, sturdy metal skewer. Secure the breast to the prong. Slide on the second prong and attach it to the other smaller end.

5. Reposition the turkey breast in the center of the spit, and tighten the bolts on the prongs. If your rotisserie has a counterweight that fits on the spit or its handle, secure it in place. Attach the spit to the motor and turn on the power. Close the grill cover unless the manufacturer's instructions say otherwise.

6. Cook until an instant-read thermometer stuck in the thickest part of the breast reads 165° to 170°F, $1\frac{1}{2}$ to 2 hours, depending on the size of the breast and type of rotisserie. Don't open the grill too often or you will increase the cooking time substantially.

7. With heatproof mitts, remove the spit from the grill. Unscrew the counterweight and bolts, and slide the turkey breast and prongs off. Set the turkey breast on a large cutting board. Pull off the prongs. Tent the turkey breast loosely with foil. Let it sit about 10 minutes, so the juices can settle, then carve and serve.

GRILLING TIP

Flavoring pastes, which are basically wet versions of a dry rub, work great with turkey breast. Just slather the paste on and under the skin an hour or two before you begin cooking. For starters, try these:

- Combine $\frac{1}{2}$ cup fresh thyme leaves, $\frac{1}{2}$ cup fresh flat-leaf parsley leaves, 4 peeled garlic cloves, 2 teaspoons kosher salt or coarse sea salt, and $\frac{1}{2}$ cup extra-virgin olive oil in a blender or food processor and puree until smooth.

- Combine one 3.5-ounce package Mexican achiote paste (in the Hispanic section of the supermarket), 2 peeled garlic cloves, $\frac{1}{3}$ cup orange juice, and 1 tablespoon fresh lime juice in a blender and puree until smooth.

- Combine $\frac{1}{2}$ cup fresh rosemary leaves and $\frac{1}{2}$ cup extra-virgin olive oil in a small bowl. Let steep for 5 minutes, then strain the oil, discarding the rosemary. Combine the oil with the grated zest and juice of 2 lemons, $\frac{1}{4}$ cup chopped onion, 1 peeled garlic clove, and 2 teaspoons kosher salt or coarse sea salt in a food processor or blender and puree until smooth.

LEG OF LAMB WITH MINT JULEP SAUCE

The English may have popularized the mating of lamb and mint, but in this recipe we take the idea in a deliciously American direction. **SERVES 8**

One 5- to 5 1/2-pound boneless leg of lamb, rolled and tied

Kosher salt or coarse sea salt

Freshly ground black pepper

MINT JULEP SAUCE
2 cups loosely packed fresh mint leaves, finely chopped

2/3 cup raspberry vinegar or other fruit vinegar

1/3 cup sugar

3 tablespoons bourbon or other American whiskey, or more to taste

Fresh mint sprigs, for garnish (optional)

1. Generously sprinkle the lamb with salt and pepper and let it sit, covered, at room temperature for about 30 minutes.

2. Whisk the sauce ingredients in a small bowl until the sugar dissolves; cover and set aside at room temperature.

3. Fire up the rotisserie, removing the spit first if it's in place, and heat the grill with the lid closed. Use the set rotisserie temperature, if your grill functions that way, or bring the heat to medium (4 to 5 seconds with the hand test).

4. Slide one of the prongs onto the far end of the spit, facing toward the center. Next slide on the lamb, running the spit through the center and working it through the meat. Secure the first end to the prong. Slide on the second prong and attach it to the other end of the meat.

5. Reposition the lamb in the center of the spit and tighten the bolts on the prongs. If your rotisserie has a counterweight that fits on the spit or its handle, secure it in place. Attach the spit to the motor and turn on the power. Place a shallow drip pan

under the lamb to catch the drippings. (If your rotisserie sits directly over the fire, keep the pan as small as possible to avoid blocking much of the heat. This may increase the projected cooking time by a few minutes.) Close the grill cover unless the manufacturer's instructions say otherwise.

6. Cook until well browned, 45 to 60 minutes, depending on the mass of the lamb and the type of rotisserie. Baste once with the drippings after about 30 minutes. Don't open the grill too many other times or you will increase the cooking time substantially. Check the meat in several places with an instant-read thermometer. We prefer the meat with sections done at least to a very rare 112°F and up to about 128°F, which will look cooked through but still remain juicy.

7. With heatproof mitts, remove the spit from the grill. Unscrew the counterweight and bolts, and slide the lamb and prongs off. Set the lamb on a large cutting board. Pull off the prongs. Tent loosely with foil and let sit for about 10 minutes, so the juices can settle. Degrease the warm pan drippings to serve along with the lamb if you wish.

8. Snip off the twine or netting. Slice thinly across the muscle grain, changing directions as the grain changes. Garnish with fresh mint sprigs, if you wish. Serve, passing the sauce and the degreased pan drippings, if you wish, on the side.

take the idea in a deliciously American direction

ROSEMARY-SCENTED PORK LOIN

If you haven't done it before, this is the time to seek out a Kurobuta, Berkshire, or other heritage pork loin. Spit-roasting the meat brings out its natural flavor, which is always superior in a well-marbled heritage cut. **SERVES 6**

One 3-pound boneless pork loin roast, preferably Kurobuta or other heritage pork, any surface fat left on

1 bunch fresh rosemary, about 8 stalks at least 4 inches in length, plus more for garnish, if desired

1 tablespoon chopped garlic

2 teaspoons smoked salt, hickory salt, kosher salt, or coarse sea salt

1. At least 1^1/$_2$ hours and up to 24 hours before you plan to roast the pork loin, season it. Pull a few little sprigs of the rosemary off the branches. Poke the branches through the pork loin from end to end, spacing them somewhat evenly. Into the holes created by the rosemary, or any natural small pockets in the meat, push the remaining rosemary sprigs. Rub down the meat with the garlic and salt, again poking it into any crevices or cavities.

2. Place the meat in a large zipper-top plastic bag, seal, and refrigerate until shortly before you plan to cook. Then let it sit at room temperature for 30 minutes before proceeding.

3. Fire up the rotisserie, removing the spit first if it's in place, and heat the grill with the lid closed. Use the set rotisserie temperature, if your grill functions that way, or bring the heat to medium (4 to 5 seconds with the hand test).

4. Slide one of the prongs onto the far end of the spit, facing toward the center. Next slide on the pork loin, using the spit's tip to begin running the roast onto the spit. Try to thread it on with the spit going directly through the center. Secure the end of the meat to the first prong. Now slide on the second prong and attach it to the other end of the meat.

5. Reposition the meat in the center of the spit, and tighten the bolts on the prongs. If your rotisserie has a counterweight that fits in the spit or its handle, secure it in place. Attach the spit to the motor and turn on the power. Place a shallow drip pan under the roast to catch the drippings. (If your rotisserie sits directly over the fire, keep the pan as small as possible to avoid blocking much of the heat. This may increase the projected cooking time by a few minutes.) Close the grill cover unless the manufacturer's instructions say otherwise.

6. Cook until an instant-read thermometer inserted deep in the loin reads 155° to 160°F, 1 1/4 to 1 1/2 hours, depending on the rotisserie and the thickness and density of the meat. About halfway through the cooking, baste once with the pan drippings. (If there are hardly any, use a few tablespoons of melted butter or extra-virgin olive oil instead, then baste a second time about 15 minutes later.) Don't open the grill too many other times or you will increase the cooking time substantially.

7. With heatproof mitts, remove the spit from the grill. Unscrew the counterweight and bolts, and slide the pork and prongs off. Set the meat on a large cutting board. Pull off the prongs. Tent loosely with foil and let sit for 10 minutes, so the juices can settle, then carve into thin slices. Degrease the warm pan drippings to serve along with the meat if you wish, and drizzle them over the pork slices. If the holes the spit leaves in the slices bother you, disguise them with a few more rosemary sprigs.

PORK LOIN AL PASTOR

If you've ever eaten a Mexican taco *al pastor*, it was cooked in a manner similar to this, though probably on a vertical rotisserie, which is more common in commercial kitchens. You can serve slices of this pork loin in tacos, if you wish, or for a fancier presentation just carve it at the table like other roasts and offer the tortillas and onion-pineapple relish on the side. **SERVES 8 TO 12**

RECADO MARINADE

1/4 cup lightly packed garlic cloves, pan-roasted in a dry skillet over medium heat until lightly browned and soft, then peeled

1 red-ripe plum tomato, pan-roasted in a dry skillet over high heat until soft, blistered, and deeply browned

2 tablespoons extra-virgin olive oil

2 tablespoons achiote paste (look for it in the Hispanic section of the supermarket)

2 tablespoons ground dried mild to medium red chile, such as ancho, New Mexican, or guajillo

2 teaspoons kosher salt or coarse sea salt

One 4-pound boneless pork loin roast, tied

1 small pineapple, peeled and cut in half across

2 medium-size white onions, peeled

Top-quality extra-virgin olive oil

At least 2 dozen corn tortillas, warmed

1. At least 4 hours and up to 24 hours before you plan to cook the pork loin, puree the *recado* marinade ingredients in a blender or food processor.

2. Place the pork in a large zipper-top plastic bag, then rub the *recado* marinade all over it, pushing it into the cracks and crevices, too. Pull the bag up over the pork and seal. Refrigerate until about 30 minutes before you plan to cook.

3. Oil the pineapple and onions and set aside.

4. Fire up the rotisserie, removing the spit first if it's in place, and heat the grill with the lid closed. Use the set rotisserie temperature, if your grill functions that way, or bring the heat to medium (4 to 5 seconds with the hand test).

5. Slide one of the prongs onto the far end of the spit, points facing toward the center. Next slide on one of the onions and one of the pineapple sections, using the spit's tip to run them onto the spit, then securing them with the prongs. Next slide on the pork loin. Try to thread it on with the spit going directly through the center. Secure the meat to the prong. Slide on the other pineapple section, followed by the second onion. Slide on the second prong with points facing the food and attach it to that end.

6. Reposition the meat in the center of the spit, with the onions and pineapple chunks snugly against both ends, and tighten the bolts on the prongs. If your rotisserie has a counterweight that fits on the spit or its handle, secure it in place. Place a shallow drip pan under the roast to catch the drippings. (If your rotisserie sits directly over the fire, keep the pan as small as possible to avoid blocking much of the heat. This may increase the projected cooking time by a few minutes.) Attach the spit to the motor and turn on the power. Close the grill cover unless the manufacturer's instructions say otherwise.

7. Cook until an instant-read thermometer inserted in the center of the meat records an internal temperature of 155° to 160°F. The *recado* will be charred in some spots and deeply browned in others. About halfway through the cooking, baste once with the pan drippings. (If there are hardly any, use a few additional tablespoons of extra-virgin olive oil instead, then baste a second time about 15 minutes later.) Don't open the grill too many other times or you will increase the cooking time substantially.

8. With heatproof mitts, remove the spit from the grill. Unscrew the counterweight and bolts, and slide off the food and the prongs. Set the meat on a large cutting board. Pull off the prongs. Let the meat sit, tented loosely with foil, for about 10 minutes, so the juices can settle.

9. Core the pineapple. Chop the onion and pineapple together into bite-size pieces. Carve the meat into thin slices. Serve with or on tortillas, along with the onion-pineapple relish.

FIRED-UP FISH

69

SIMPLE, SUMPTUOUS POMPANO

Mid-twentieth-century cookbook author Sheila Hibben once described pompano as "the perfection of fish—and perhaps of all food." It's widely known and loved in Florida, but deserves much more renown in the rest of the country. Small snappers can fill in for the pompano, though we agree with Hibben that nothing really matches it. **SERVES 4**

> Four 1- to 1¹/₄-pound or two 1³/₄- to 2-pound pompano, gutted
>
> Vegetable oil or extra-virgin olive oil
>
> Grated zest and juice of 1 lemon
>
> 1 small onion, sliced very thin
>
> Kosher salt or coarse sea salt
>
> Freshly ground black pepper
>
> Lemon wedges and fresh mint sprigs, for garnish

1. Cut 2 or 3 moderately deep diagonal slashes into both sides of each fish. Rub each fish inside and out with a thin coat of oil. Sprinkle the cavities of each fish with the lemon zest and juice and onion, and season to taste with salt and pepper.

2. Fire up the grill, bringing the temperature to medium-high heat (2 to 3 seconds with the hand test). Oil the cooking grate.

3. Arrange the fish on the grill with the tails angled away from the hottest part of the fire. Grill, uncovered, for 9 to 10 minutes per inch of thickness, turning once, until opaque throughout. To turn the fish, roll them over gently rather than lifting them up and flipping them. If you feel any resistance when you turn the fish, re-oil the grate.

4. Brush the top of each fish lightly with oil for a shinier appearance. Transfer the fish to a platter and garnish with lemon wedges and mint.

FISHING FOR COMPLIMENTS

Grilling is a splendid way to cook many fish, perhaps the best method overall for enhancing innate flavor. Whole fish should weigh under 3 pounds and measure no thicker than 1½ inches at their most portly point. Using medium-high heat gets the right surface sear while allowing the center to cook through before the skin burns. Good candidates for grilling whole include pompano (see page 166), sea bass or striped bass, small bluefish, snapper, and trout.

With fillets and steaks, make sure they're freshly cut and preferably just under 1 inch thick. Salmon, shark, and tuna grill well on a hot fire, but halibut, mahi-mahi, and swordfish do better on medium-high. When grilling any fish, be sure to keep the cooking grate especially clean and well oiled, to avoid leaving behind a chunk of your dinner. Use a thin-bladed spatula, rather than tongs, to turn fish.

We give visual cues about fish doneness in each of our recipes. The principle varies a bit depending upon whether the fish is meaty or flaky. We think some fish, like salmon and tuna, are at their best when seared well on the surface but before they are cooked all the way through. You can always leave yours over the fire a bit longer if you wish.

70

BASIL-SCENTED SALMON

We love fresh basil with salmon. For grilling ask your fish market for center-cut fillet sections, which are the meatiest and don't taper as much as those from other parts of the salmon. If necessary, take off thinner pieces while thicker ones remain on the grill, and whisk off fillets sooner for those who prefer it less done. Whenever possible we suggest opting for wild Pacific salmon.
SERVES 4 TO 6

Four to six 3/4-inch-thick skin-on salmon fillet sections (5 to 6 ounces each)

MARINADE
1/2 cup orange juice
1/2 teaspoon kosher salt or coarse sea salt

BASIL OIL
1/2 cup lightly packed fresh basil leaves
1/2 cup top-quality extra-virgin olive oil
1/2 teaspoon kosher salt or coarse sea salt

Flaky sea salt (such as Maldon), kosher salt, or coarse sea salt
Fresh basil sprigs, for garnish (optional)

1. Stroke the surface of the salmon, feeling for tiny pin bones. Use tweezers to remove any that you find.

2. Prepare the marinade, first pouring the orange juice into a shallow dish that will hold all the fillets in a single layer. Stir in the salt, then add the fillets, skin side up. Let sit at room temperature for 15 to 30 minutes.

3. Puree the basil oil ingredients together in a food processor or blender. Measure out 2 tablespoons of the oil and reserve the rest.

4. Fire up the grill, bringing the temperature to high (1 to 2 seconds with the hand test). Oil the cooking grate.

5. Drain the salmon, discarding the marinade. Brush the flesh side of the fillets lightly with the reserved 2 tablespoons of basil oil.

6. Transfer the fillets skin side up to the grate. Grill, uncovered, for 2 minutes, rotating the fillets a half turn after 1 minute for crisscross grill marks. (If the fillets are thicker than 1 inch, keep them skin side up for an additional minute, rotating after 1 1/2 minutes.) Don't touch or move the fillets except when it's time to rotate or turn, because getting a good sear where the fish touches the grate is essential to help prevent sticking. If you get any resistance when you rotate the fish, re-oil the grate. Gently turn the fillets skin side down. Brush the cooked surface lightly with enough basil oil so it glistens, and continue cooking for about 4 more minutes, until the skin is brown and crisp. The salmon is done when just barely opaque, with a touch of darker translucence remaining at the center.

7. Arrange the fillets, skin side down, on plates. Drizzle the fillets equally with the remaining basil oil, letting some of it pool on the plates. Sprinkle with salt flakes and serve, garnished with basil sprigs if you wish.

71

PLANKED SALMON

If you've never tried grilling on a wood plank, don't skip over this because it sounds involved. In fact, it's one of the easiest ways to cook fish on a grill, with none of the usual concerns about the fish sticking to the cooking grate or falling apart on the way from the grill to the plate. The method works great with salmon and isn't difficult. These days you can find cooking planks in cookware and grill stores and most supermarkets, especially in the summer. We prefer thicker planks with some heft, not the tissue-thin ones. After you're done cooking, present the salmon at the table on the singed plank for the epitome in wilderness serving-ware. **SERVES 8 TO 12**

> 1 plank, preferably alder or cedar, long enough for the salmon but short enough to fit inside your grill
>
> One 1/2- to 3/4-inch-thick salmon fillet (1 1/2 to 3 pounds), skin on or off (your preference), or full side of salmon, preferably wild Pacific salmon
>
> Extra-virgin olive oil
>
> Flaky sea salt (such as Maldon), kosher salt, or coarse sea salt
>
> Cracked pink peppercorns or freshly ground black pepper
>
> Top-quality extra-virgin olive oil (optional)

1. Soak the plank in water, at least 30 minutes for a one-time-use plank, and up to 2 hours for a 1/2- to 1-inch-thick board. Weight it down with a can of tomatoes if it wants to float.

2. Stroke the surface of the salmon, feeling for tiny pin bones. Use tweezers to remove any that you find. Coat the surface with oil and then season generously with salt and pepper. Cover the salmon and let it sit at room temperature for about 30 minutes.

3. Fire up the grill, bringing the temperature to medium-high (3 seconds with the hand test). Have a spray bottle of water handy.

4. Transfer the salmon to the plank, skin side down if there is skin. Place the plank in the center of the grill and close the grill cover, to hold in the smoke from the smoldering wood. (Yes, this is one of the few times we close a grill cover while cooking.) Cook for 8 to 10 minutes. You should see a light plume of smoke during most of the cooking process. If you see a billowing dark cloud emerging, or any other sign that the board is burning instead of simply smoking, open the grill carefully and douse any flames with your spray bottle.

5. Turn off the grill if using gas, or shut down the vents of a charcoal grill, and let the salmon sit in the covered grill 8 to 10 minutes longer. The plank helps shield the salmon from the heat, making the cooking time longer than if you were cooking it directly over the fire. The salmon is done when just barely opaque throughout, with a touch of darker translucence remaining at the center. The smoke will brown the surface, and the high heat will nicely crisp it, an effect enhanced by the coarse seasonings.

6. Use a pair of washable heatproof mitts to remove the plank with the salmon from the grill. Transfer the plank to an upside-down baking sheet placed on a work surface nearest the grill. The bottom of the plank will be sooty, so be careful about what you put it on, even after it's cooled.

7. Definitely show off your salmon on the plank before divvying it up. The easiest way to serve is to bring the plates to the plank. If you want to serve the salmon at the table, cover the baking sheet with a washable large cloth napkin or other fabric that can be cleaned easily. Then place the plank with the salmon on the napkin and take the whole thing to the table to serve.

8. Be sure to let the plank cool completely or submerge it in water before you think about stashing it somewhere or tossing it out; it takes only one persistent ember to start a fire.

72

SUMMERY SALMON SANDWICH

It couldn't be coincidental that wild salmon and great garden produce flourish at the same time of the year. A feast of summer flavors, this sandwich deserves an honored spot at any outdoor brunch or dinner. **SERVES 4**

DILL PASTE

1/4 cup minced fresh dill

2 teaspoons vegetable oil

1 teaspoon kosher salt or coarse sea salt

1 teaspoon freshly ground black pepper

Four 1/2- to 3/4-inch thick skin-on salmon fillet sections (5 to 6 ounces each)

3 slices bacon, chopped

1 small red onion, slivered

DILL MAYONNAISE

1/4 cup mayonnaise

1 1/2 tablespoons minced fresh dill

2 teaspoons top-quality extra-virgin olive oil

8 thin slices sturdy sourdough or semolina bread

Red-ripe tomato slices

Lettuce leaves

1. At least 1 hour and up to 4 hours before you plan to grill the salmon fillets, combine the dill paste ingredients in a small bowl. Rub the paste all over the salmon fillets, cover them, and refrigerate.

2. In a small skillet, fry the bacon until brown and crisp. With a slotted spoon, transfer the bacon to a double layer of paper towels. Sauté the onion in the bacon drippings over medium heat until soft. With a slotted spoon, transfer the onion to the paper towels next to the bacon.

3. Remove the salmon from the refrigerator and let it sit, covered, for about 20 minutes.

4. Stir together the dill mayonnaise ingredients and set aside.

5. Fire up the grill, bringing the temperature to high (1 to 2 seconds with the hand test). Oil the cooking grate.

6. Transfer the fillets skin side up to the grate. Grill, uncovered, for 2 minutes, rotating the fillets a half turn after 1 minute for crisscross grill marks. Don't touch or move the fillets except when it's time to rotate or turn, because getting a good sear where the fish touches the grate is essential to help prevent sticking. If you get any resistance when you rotate the fish, re-oil the grate. Gently turn the fillets skin side down. The salmon is done when just barely opaque, with a touch of darker translucence remaining at the center. Toast the bread slices on the edge of the grill in the last few minutes.

7. Carefully strip the skin off the bottom of each salmon fillet. Slather the mayonnaise over one side of each slice of toasted bread. Place a salmon fillet section on each of 4 slices of bread. Spoon equal portions of sautéed onion over the fish, followed by equal portions of bacon, tomato slices, and lettuce. Top each sandwich with one of the remaining slices of bread. Serve immediately.

a feast of summer flavors, this sandwich deserves an honored spot at any outdoor brunch or dinner

A STEAK-LOVER'S TUNA STEAK

Grill and dress tuna as you would a fine beefsteak and it will shine in the same way. Like a prime rib-eye, coat a tuna steak with pepper, cook it over a two-level fire until it's just warmed through and still red or pink in the center, and crown it at the table with a dollop of creamy horseradish sauce. A sure bet as a top 100 choice for us—this even makes our top 10! **SERVES 4**

LEMON-PEPPER PASTE

1 tablespoon fresh lemon juice

1^1/$_2$ teaspoons vegetable oil

1^1/$_2$ teaspoons coarsely ground black pepper

^{1}/$_2$ teaspoon kosher salt or coarse sea salt

Two 1-inch-thick tuna steaks (about 1 pound each)

HORSERADISH CREAM

^{1}/$_2$ cup sour cream

1 tablespoon prepared horseradish

2 teaspoons grated mild onion

^{1}/$_4$ teaspoon kosher salt or coarse sea salt

1. At least 1 hour and up to 4 hours before you plan to grill the tuna steaks, combine the lemon-pepper paste, ingredients in a small bowl. The mixture will be very wet. Cut each tuna steak in half crosswise so that you have four 1-inch-thick portions. Coat the steaks all over with the paste, cover them, and refrigerate.

2. Stir together the horseradish cream ingredients in a small serving bowl. Cover and refrigerate until needed.

3. Remove the tuna from the refrigerator and let it sit, covered, at room temperature for about 30 minutes. Blot any accumulated liquid from the surface of the steaks.

4. Fire up the grill for a two-level fire capable of cooking at the same time on both high heat (1 to 2 seconds with the hand test) and medium heat (4 to 5 seconds with the hand test); see page 6. Oil the cooking grate.

5. Transfer the steaks to the grate and grill, uncovered, over high heat for 2 minutes per side. Don't touch or move the steaks except when it's time to turn, because getting a good sear where the fish touches the grate is essential to help prevent sticking. If you get any resistance when you turn the fish, re-oil the grate. Move to medium heat and continue cooking for another 2 to 3 minutes per side, leaving a distinctly pink center.

6. Serve the steaks immediately, with dollops of the horseradish cream.

GRILLING TIP

When we're serving 8-ounce fish steak portions, as we suggest in our tuna and swordfish recipes, we buy thick 1-pound cuts and then halve them at home. If you ask a market for portions smaller than a 1/2 pound, they're likely to slice the fish steaks too thin. Then you end up with an overcooked interior by the time the outside has seared well.

DRY-RUBBED TUNA STEAKS

Many dry rubs work as well on tuna as they do on meat. In this case, a dry rub of fennel seeds and lemon zest provides a simple but savory coat for tuna steaks. **SERVES 4**

DRY RUB

1 tablespoon crushed fennel seeds

1 tablespoon minced lemon zest

3/4 teaspoon kosher salt or coarse sea salt

Two 1-inch-thick tuna steaks (about 1 pound each)

Olive oil spray, preferably, or vegetable oil spray

Lemon wedges, for garnish

Fresh feathery fennel tops, for garnish (optional)

1. At least 1 hour and up to 4 hours before you plan to grill the tuna, combine the dry rub ingredients in a small bowl. Cut each tuna steak in half crosswise so that you have four 1-inch-thick portions. Rub the steaks all over with the dry rub, cover them, and refrigerate.

2. Remove the steaks from the refrigerator and let them sit, covered, at room temperature for about 30 minutes.

3. Fire up the grill for a two-level fire capable of cooking at the same time on both high heat (1 to 2 seconds with the hand test) and medium heat (4 to 5 seconds with the hand test); see page 6. Oil the cooking grate.

4. Just before grilling, spritz the steaks thoroughly with oil. Transfer the steaks to the grate and grill, uncovered, over high heat for 2 minutes per side. Don't touch or move the steaks except when it's time to turn, because getting a good sear where the fish touches the grate is essential to help prevent sticking. If you get any resistance when you turn the fish, re-oil the grate. Move the tuna to medium heat and continue cooking for another 2 to 3 minutes per side, leaving a distinctly pink center.

5. Serve the steaks immediately, with lemon wedges and, if you wish, fennel tops.

SALMON-BUTTERED HALIBUT STEAKS

Halibut steaks taste similar to their swordfish counterparts, but seem to us to have a deeper inherent flavor. We minimize the seasoning for them, here using a smoked-salmon butter and caper garnish. **SERVES 4**

SMOKED SALMON BUTTER

6 tablespoons (3/4 stick) unsalted butter

3 ounces cold-smoked salmon, minced

Grated zest and juice of 1 small lemon

One 1-inch thick halibut steak (1^{1}/$_{2}$ to 1^{3}/$_{4}$ pounds)

Extra-virgin olive oil

Kosher salt or coarse sea salt

Capers or caper berries, for garnish

1. In a small skillet, melt the butter over medium-low heat. Remove from the heat and add the salmon. With the back of a fork, mash the salmon until nearly dissolved in the butter. Stir in the lemon zest and juice. (The butter can be made a day or two ahead and refrigerated or kept frozen for several weeks. Reheat it before proceeding.)

2. Cut around the center bone of the halibut steak to make 4 medallions. Coat the fish lightly with oil and sprinkle it with salt. Let it sit, covered, at room temperature for about 20 minutes. Meanwhile, fire up the grill, bringing the temperature to medium-high (3 seconds with the hand test). Oil the cooking grate.

3. Transfer the halibut to the grate and grill, uncovered, turning once, until opaque throughout, 8 to 10 minutes. Rotate the fish a half turn once on each side. Don't touch or move the fish except when it's time to turn or rotate, because getting a good sear where the fish touches the grate is essential to help prevent sticking. If there is any resistance when you turn or rotate the fish, re-oil the grate.

4. Serve the halibut hot, topped with the smoked salmon butter and a scattering of capers.

SWORDFISH STEAKS WITH TOMATILLO VINAIGRETTE

Swordfish is meaty like tuna, but it requires an adjustment in grilling technique. For the best result, switch to a steady medium-high fire. In this case, we apply a dry rub to the fish first and finish it off with a tangy dressing. **SERVES 4**

DRY RUB

2 tablespoons ground coriander

1 tablespoon smoked sweet paprika

2 teaspoons kosher salt or coarse sea salt

1 teaspoon ground cumin

Two 1-inch-thick swordfish steaks (about 3/4 pound each)

TOMATILLO VINAIGRETTE

4 ounces fresh tomatillos (about 4 medium), husked and rinsed

1/4 cup vegetable oil

1 tablespoon minced onion

1 tablespoon fresh lime juice

1/2 fresh or pickled jalapeño, seeded and minced

1/8 teaspoon kosher salt or coarse sea salt

Vegetable oil spray

Diced red-ripe tomato, for garnish (optional)

1. At least 1 hour and up to 4 hours before you plan to grill the swordfish, combine the dry rub ingredients in a small bowl. Cut each swordfish steak in half crosswise so that you have four 1-inch-thick portions. Rub the steaks all over with the mixture, cover them, and refrigerate.

2. Shortly before you plan to grill, puree the vinaigrette ingredients together in a food processor; set aside.

3. Remove the steaks from the refrigerator and let them sit, covered, at room temperature for about 30 minutes.

4. Fire up the grill, bringing the temperature to medium-high (3 seconds with the hand test). Oil the cooking grate.

5. Just before grilling, spritz the steaks thoroughly with oil. Transfer the steaks to the grate and grill, uncovered, for 4 to 5 minutes per side, until opaque throughout. Rotate the fish a half turn once on each side. Don't touch or move the steaks except when it's time to turn or rotate, because getting a good sear where the fish touches the grate is essential to help prevent sticking. If there is any resistance when you turn or rotate the fish, re-oil the grate.

6. Serve the steaks hot, drizzled with the vinaigrette. Drop a few tomato bits over each serving for a little added color, if you wish.

apply a dry rub to the fish before grilling and finish it off with a tangy dressing

TANGERINE-TERIYAKI HALIBUT FILLETS

Halibut, being a firm, meaty fish, can handle grilling and also stand up to the addition of a robust Japanese-inspired sauce. **SERVES 4**

TANGERINE-TERIYAKI SAUCE

1/4 cup mirin (see Grilling Tip on page 181)

2 tablespoons sake or dry sherry

2 tablespoons soy sauce, preferably not a low-sodium variety

2 tablespoons fresh tangerine juice or orange juice

1 tablespoon minced fresh ginger

1 teaspoon sugar

Four 1-inch-thick skinless halibut fillets (about 6 ounces each)

Vegetable oil spray

1. To prepare the sauce, first warm the mirin and sake in a small saucepan over medium-low heat for 5 minutes. Stir in the soy sauce and continue heating until reduced by about half, another 5 to 8 minutes. Add the remaining ingredients, stirring until the sugar dissolves. (The sauce can be made up to a week ahead, covered, and refrigerated.)

2. Fire up the grill, bringing the temperature to medium-high (3 seconds with the hand test). Oil the cooking grate.

3. Just before grilling, spritz the fillets with oil. Transfer the fillets to the grate and grill, uncovered, turning three times, until opaque throughout, 8 to 10 minutes. Rotate the fish a half turn once on each side. Don't touch or move the fillets except when it's time to rotate or turn, because getting a good sear where the fish touches the grate is essential to help prevent sticking. If there is any resistance when you turn or rotate the fish, re-oil the grate. As soon as a cooked side of a fillet is turned up, brush it with the teriyaki sauce so that it glazes and nearly lacquers the surfaces.

4. Brush the fillets generously with any remaining teriyaki sauce before serving.

a firm, meaty fish can handle grilling and also stand up to the addition of a robust Japanese-inspired sauce

CATFISH WITH SNAPPY TARTAR SAUCE

Most people get their catfish crispy by deep-frying it. The rub in this recipe allows you to achieve some of the same crusty surface through grilling. After much experimentation, we feel that catfish on the grill comes out best when it is turned to face the fire twice on one side, but only once on the other. The fish cooks through but doesn't start to break apart. Add your own homemade tartar sauce, zipped up with a little jalapeño, to enhance the result. **SERVES 4**

TARTAR SAUCE

1 cup mayonnaise

1 tablespoon minced pickled jalapeño

2 teaspoons small capers or minced large capers

2 teaspoons minced fresh dill or 1 teaspoon dried dill weed

1 teaspoon fresh lemon juice

1/4 teaspoon Dijon mustard

DRY RUB

1 1/2 tablespoons celery salt

1 1/2 teaspoons freshly ground black pepper

1 1/2 teaspoons sweet paprika

1/8 teaspoon cayenne pepper

Four 3/4-inch-thick catfish fillets (8 to 10 ounces each)

Vegetable oil spray

1. Mix the tartar sauce ingredients in a small bowl. Cover and refrigerate the mixture for at least 30 minutes or up to 24 hours.

2. Combine the dry rub ingredients in a small bowl. Coat the catfish all over with the rub. Cover the catfish and let it sit at room temperature for 20 to 30 minutes.

3. Fire up the grill, bringing the temperature to medium-high to high (2 to 3 seconds with the hand test).

4. Just before grilling, spritz the fillets with oil. Transfer the fillets to a well-oiled cooking grate or, preferably, to a hinged grill basket or well-oiled small-mesh grill rack placed on the cooking grate. Grill, uncovered, for 7 to 9 minutes, carefully turning twice so that one side crisps a bit more than the other. Rotate the fillets 180 degrees when they are turned back onto the side that was grilled previously. The fish is done when flaky and opaque.

5. Serve immediately with the crisper side up, accompanied by the tartar sauce.

GRILLING TIP

Spray oil is an easy and efficient way to coat fish for grilling. Just don't squirt it onto a grate that's above a live fire unless singed hair is fashionable in your neighborhood. It's better to heat the grate and then carefully brush it with oil, allowing any flare-ups to recede before you proceed. If you re-oil the grate during the cooking, be cautious to avoid drips into the fire.

SUCCULENT SHELLFISH

LOUISIANA BARBECUED SHRIMP

If you've tried barbecued shrimp in New Orleans, you know it's not really barbecued, but it is absolutely delectable. This is a grilled version of that local favorite, usually skillet-cooked and full of the fiery flavors of black pepper and Louisiana hot sauce. If you own a mesh pan to use on the grill, this is a great time to pull it out. **SERVES 4**

MARINADE

1/2 cup Worcestershire sauce

3 tablespoons tomato-based barbecue sauce

1 tablespoon minced onion

2 garlic cloves, minced

1 tablespoon cracked black peppercorns

1 teaspoon kosher salt or coarse sea salt

1/4 teaspoon Tabasco or other Louisiana hot pepper sauce, or more to taste

1 1/2 pounds medium to large shrimp, peeled and, if you wish, deveined

3 tablespoons unsalted butter, in several chunks

2 tablespoons fresh lemon juice

1. Whisk together the marinade ingredients in a large bowl. Stir in the shrimp and let them soak in the mixture for 30 minutes, stirring occasionally.

2. Fire up the grill, bringing the temperature to high (1 to 2 seconds with hand test).

3. Drain the marinade from the shrimp into a medium-size saucepan. Bring the marinade to a boil and boil vigorously for several minutes. Add the butter, whisking until it melts completely. Remove from the heat and stir in the lemon juice. Reserve to use as a sauce.

4. Place the shrimp in a mesh grill pan or in a single layer on a well-oiled small-mesh grill rack placed on the cooking grate. Grill the shrimp, uncovered, for 2 to 3 minutes, brush with the sauce, then stir around in the pan or turn on the rack, and grill for 2 to 3 minutes more on the second side. The shrimp are done when they are opaque, with a few lightly browned edges.

5. Arrange the shrimp on a large platter or on individual plates, pour the remaining sauce over them, and serve right away.

a local favorite, usually skillet-cooked and full of the fiery flavors of black pepper and Louisiana hot sauce

SKEWERED SHRIMP WITH ROMESCO SAUCE

What New Orleans cooks can do with barbecue sauce may be rivaled only by what the Spanish can do with romesco sauce. Sure, you can use a bottled commercial version of the sauce in this recipe, but our homemade version will show you just how luscious romesco can be. **SERVES 4**

ROMESCO SAUCE

One 4-ounce jar piquillo peppers, with their juice, *or* one 4-ounce jar pimientos, preferably fire-roasted, with their juice, plus 1/4 to 1/2 teaspoon crushed red pepper

One 1-ounce slice chewy country bread, toasted or grilled and torn into several pieces

1/4 cup salted almonds, preferably Marcona, toasted in a dry skillet over medium heat until fragrant

1 red-ripe plum tomato, cut into several pieces

2 plump garlic cloves, peeled

1 tablespoon Spanish hot paprika

1 tablespoon sherry vinegar or red wine vinegar

1 tablespoon warm water

6 to 8 tablespoons top-quality extra-virgin olive oil

Kosher salt or coarse sea salt

1 1/2 pounds medium to large shrimp, peeled and, if you wish, deveined

16 metal or soaked bamboo skewers

1. Prepare the romesco sauce. In a food processor, combine the piquillos and juice, bread, almonds, tomato, garlic, paprika, vinegar, and warm water. Process until a thick puree forms. With the motor running, pour in enough of the oil to make the sauce smooth and easily spoonable. Add a pinch or two of salt, as needed. Let the

sauce sit at room temperature for up to 30 minutes or cover and refrigerate for up to several days.

2. Spoon half of the romesco sauce into a small bowl and reserve it. Toss the shrimp with the remaining romesco sauce and let them sit at room temperature for about 15 minutes.

3. Thread the shrimp onto the skewers. Hold a shrimp so that its two ends make a lazy "U" and then thread two side-by-side skewers up through the middle of each shrimp. Repeat with the remaining shrimp, making 8 kebobs.

4. Fire up the grill, bringing the temperature to high (1 to 2 seconds with the hand test). Arrange the skewers on the grill so that the handles angle away from the heat. Grill the skewers, uncovered, for about 2 minutes per side, turning once. The shrimp are done when just firm, opaque, and pink-white, with a few lightly browned edges. Serve hot or chilled with the reserved bowl of romesco sauce.

SEAFOOD PAELLA WITH ALLIOLI

You can prepare paella in a large skillet, but if you decide you like it as much as we do, do yourself a favor and get a real paella pan from a local kitchen store or perhaps www.spanishtable.com. A 14-inch pan is perfect for this recipe. Also, for premier flavor, use the best available stock in paella, preferably homemade or at least a good store-bought version. The recipe contains a little pork for flavoring, but it can be left out if your diners don't eat meat. The accompanying *allioli* is the Spanish version of the French aioli, or garlicky mayo. No one else will know if you decide not to make it, but you will get kudos if you do. This is our favorite party dish, so we've increased the serving size to accommodate a small crowd. **SERVES 8 TO 10**

ALLIOLI
4 to 6 plump garlic cloves, chopped by hand

1 1/2 teaspoons kosher salt or coarse sea salt

2 large egg yolks, at room temperature

2 tablespoons fresh lemon juice

1 cup extra-virgin olive oil

1/4 cup vegetable oil

1 pound medium shrimp, peeled and, if you wish, deveined

1/2 pound cleaned small squid, preferably about 3 inches long, tentacles and tubes separated, or 1/2 pound squid steaks

Top-quality extra-virgin olive oil

Kosher salt or coarse sea salt

Freshly ground black pepper

16 hard-shell clams (such as cherrystones or littlenecks) or mussels, cleaned

RICE

4 cups low-sodium chicken stock

2 cups seafood stock or bottled clam juice

1 1/2 teaspoons crumbled saffron threads

1/4 cup top-quality extra-virgin olive oil

4 ounces Spanish chorizo or pancetta, chopped

1 medium-size red onion, diced

1 medium-size red bell pepper, seeded and diced

1 medium-size green bell pepper, seeded and diced

2 tablespoons minced garlic

3 cups short-grain rice, such as Bomba or Arborio

Kosher salt or coarse sea salt

1/2 cup fresh or frozen baby peas

3/4 cup pitted briny green or black olives, or a combination

1/3 cup minced fresh flat-leaf parsley

1. Prepare the *allioli*. Using a wooden spoon, mash the garlic together with the salt in a medium-size bowl. Add the egg yolks and whisk until they lighten to a pale yellow. Whisk in the lemon juice. When the mixture is frothy, continue whisking while gradually adding the oils in a steady stream until a mayonnaise consistency is reached. Taste and adjust the seasonings if necessary, cover, and refrigerate until serving time. Although *allioli* is best the day it's made, it will keep, tightly covered, for up to 2 days.

2. Fire up the grill, bringing the temperature to high (1 to 2 seconds with the hand test). If you plan to cook the rice over the grill fire, instead of on a side burner or stovetop, you'll need the capability for medium heat (4 to 5 seconds with the hand test) and medium-low heat (5 to 6 seconds) as well; see page 6.

3. Rub the shrimp and squid lightly with oil and season with salt and pepper. Cover and let sit at room temperature, along with the clams, while you start the rice.

4. Stir together the stocks and saffron and let the mixture stand. Warm the oil in a 12- to 14-inch paella pan or skillet over medium heat. Stir in the chorizo, onion, bell peppers, and garlic, and sauté several minutes, until the chorizo begins to crisp

and the vegetables are just tender. Stir in the rice and cook until translucent, 4 to 5 minutes. Give the saffron stock a stir and pour it over the rice. Add salt to taste. Cook the rice over medium-low heat, uncovered, without stirring, until the liquid is absorbed, about 20 minutes. After about 15 minutes of cooking, insert a spoon or spatula straight down into the rice in several places to make sure that the rice isn't browning on the bottom in one spot before the liquid is absorbed in others. Shift the position of the pan over the heat if it is getting more done in one spot than others. When done, the liquid should be absorbed and the rice should be tender but have the barest hint of crust on the bottom and sides.

5. When the rice has about 10 minutes to go, arrange the clams on the grill and cook on high heat until they pop open wide, 8 to 10 minutes. (Discard any that refuse to open within a couple of minutes of the others.) Remove them from the grill carefully to avoid losing the juices in the shells. Place them on top of the hot rice. Grill the shrimp and squid on a well-oiled small-mesh grill rack over high heat for a total of about 4 minutes, turning to cook on all sides. The squid tentacles will likely be ready first, so take them off as soon as they firm up. When done, the shrimp should be just firm, opaque, and pink-white, with lightly charred edges, and the squid bodies will be firm but tender. Heap the squid tentacles and shrimp over the rice. Slice the squid bodies into thin rings (or the squid steak into thin strips) and add them to the rice, too.

6. Stir the grilled seafood and peas (no need to thaw if frozen) into the rice and scatter the olives and parsley over the top. Serve immediately or cover with foil and keep warm in a low oven or on a corner of the grill. If using a paella pan, serve from the pan. If using a skillet, spoon out onto a platter and then serve. In either case, pass the *allioli* to spoon onto the warm paella.

GRILLING TIP

You can make all kinds of modifications in a dish like this. Add more of a favorite seafood, and less of one that you can't find or don't like as well. Replace one of the seafood choices with another, such as plump scallops cooked in the same fashion as the shrimp. Try using black rice instead of white for the base, which really makes the seafood stand out.

FLAME-FIRED CALAMARI

Calamari (just the fancier-sounding Italian name for squid) cooks quickly over hot flames to make a succulent seafood supper. If you like, serve it over a tangle of olive oil–tossed fettuccine. Toasted bread crumbs add texture. **SERVES 4**

BREAD CRUMBS

1/2 cup fresh country bread crumbs

1 tablespoon top-quality extra-virgin olive oil

FOR THE GRILL

11/2 pounds squid bodies, about 3 inches in length

About 1 tablespoon top-quality extra-virgin olive oil

Kosher salt or coarse sea salt

Tangy green olives, for garnish

1. Fire up the grill, bringing the temperature to high (1 to 2 seconds with the hand test). Depending on the size of the squid and the distance between the bars of your grate, you may want to place a well-oiled small-mesh grill rack over the cooking grate.

2. While the grill heats, prepare the bread crumbs. In a small skillet, stir the crumbs together with the oil. Cook briefly over medium heat, stirring occasionally, until the crumbs are toasty brown and crisp. Scrape the crumbs out onto a paper towel so that they don't continue to cook.

3. Toss the squid with just enough oil so it glistens, and season with salt to taste.

4. Transfer the squid to the grate or rack and grill, uncovered, for 3 to 4 minutes, rolling the tube-shaped bodies on all sides. The squid will go from limp to firm, and from translucent to bright white. Don't overcook or the squid will quickly resemble rubber bands. Slice across the bodies into 1/4-inch-thick rings. Arrange on plates. Sprinkle with the bread crumbs, dot each plate with several olives, and serve immediately.

83

MIMOSA-BASTED LOBSTER

Don't even think about grilling a great cold-water lobster, which tastes best boiled or steamed. For grilling, we use split tails from the warm-water, clawless spiny or rock lobster, which tastes similar to its more expensive cousin except in the richness of flavor. They are usually shipped from tropical areas already frozen, so look for them in that section of a store. Here we compensate for their diminished richness with an extravagant touch, a Champagne bath. **SERVES 4**

Two 1-pound rock lobster tails, fresh or (thawed) frozen

Vegetable oil

MIMOSA BASTE
3 tablespoons unsalted butter

Juice of 1 orange

Kosher salt or coarse sea salt

1 split (187.5 ml) Champagne or sparkling wine, at room temperature or chilled

Watercress and orange wedges, for garnish

1. Fire up the grill, bringing the temperature to medium-high (3 seconds with the hand test).

2. Place the lobster tails on a clean towel over a cutting board. The towel will help keep the lobsters from sliding as you cut them, but be careful to avoid slicing your towel. Split the lobster tails in half lengthwise with a cleaver or other heavy knife. Watch your fingers because the shells tend to be slick. Oil the shell and meat of each tail section well.

3. Prepare the mimosa baste, first melting the butter in a small saucepan over medium heat. Stir in the orange juice and a pinch of salt and remove from the heat.

4. Just before taking the lobster tails to the grill, pop open the Champagne, stir it into the butter mixture, and heat through over medium heat.

5. Transfer the lobster tails to the grill, cut sides down, and grill, uncovered, for 3 minutes. Turn them shell side down and brush the meat of each lobster thickly with the mimosa baste. Grill for another 8 to 9 minutes, until cooked through and opaque but still juicy.

6. Transfer the lobsters to a serving platter, shell side down, and spoon additional baste over them. Garnish with watercress and orange wedges and serve immediately.

rock lobster tails in an extravagant bubbly bath

84

LOBSTER BLT

This fancy and splendid-tasting triple-decker version of a BLT sandwich is suitable for almost any outdoor occasion, from a casual supper to a candlelight dinner. It's sure to be a happy surprise for all guests at the table. **SERVES 4**

Two 3/4-pound rock lobster tails, fresh or (thawed) frozen

Extra-virgin olive oil

BASTING SAUCE

3 tablespoons extra-virgin olive oil

Minced zest and juice from 1 1/2 lemons

1 teaspoon minced fresh thyme or 1/2 teaspoon dried crumbled thyme

1/2 teaspoon kosher salt or coarse sea salt

2/3 cup mayonnaise

Minced zest and juice from 1/2 lemon

Tabasco or other hot pepper sauce

12 lettuce leaves

2 red-ripe medium-size tomatoes, sliced thin

8 slices crisp-cooked bacon

12 thin but large slices country or sourdough bread, preferably cut from the center of a loaf

1. Fire up the grill, bringing the temperature to medium-high (3 seconds with the hand test).

2. Place the lobster tails on a clean towel over a cutting board. This will help keep them from sliding as you cut them, but be careful to avoid slicing your towel. Split the lobster tails in half lengthwise with a cleaver or other heavy knife. Watch your fingers because the shells tend to be slick. Oil the shell and meat of each tail section well.

3. Combine the basting sauce ingredients in a small bowl; set aside.

4. In another small bowl, stir together the mayonnaise, lemon zest and juice, and a generous splash of the Tabasco; set aside.

5. Transfer the lobster tails to the grill, cut sides down. Grill, uncovered, for 2 1/2 minutes. Turn them shell side down and baste the meat of each lobster tail generously with the basting sauce. Grill for another 6 to 8 minutes, until cooked through and opaque but still juicy. Baste again right before removing the lobster tails from the grill.

6. Transfer the lobster tails to a work surface, wait a couple of minutes until the shells become cool enough to handle, and remove the meat from each tail (using a fork works best for us). Chop the meat coarsely.

7. Spread the bread slices with the mayonnaise mixture. Cover 4 slices with half the lettuce and tomatoes and arrange the bacon equally over them. Add another bread slice to each and divide the remaining tomatoes, the lobster, and remaining lettuce between the two sandwiches. Top with the last 4 bread slices, and skewer with toothpicks if you wish. Serve warm.

85

SOFT-SHELL CRAB SALAD

When molting crabs shed their regular shells during a fleeting season, they become supremely tasty soft-shells. The quickness of the cycle boosts the price of the delicacy, but this main-dish salad spreads the cost over more dinner plates. Like most people, we often pan-fry soft-shells, but grilling makes a good alternative. Serve the salad as soon as the soft-shells come off the grill and forget any possibility of leftovers. **SERVES 4**

MUSTARD PASTE AND DRESSING

1 cup mayonnaise

1 tablespoon packed brown sugar

2 teaspoons dry mustard

2 teaspoons Worcestershire sauce

2 teaspoons steak sauce, such as A-1 Original

1 garlic clove, minced

1/8 teaspoon cayenne pepper

2 tablespoons whole or 2% milk

4 soft-shell crabs (preferably at least 3 ounces each)

5 cups shredded romaine

1 cup thinly sliced red cabbage or radicchio

4 scallions, roots and limp green tops trimmed, sliced into thin rings

1 ripe avocado, peeled, pitted, and diced

1. Mix all of the paste ingredients except the milk in a medium-size bowl. Spoon out about 3 tablespoons of the paste into a small bowl and reserve. Whisk the milk into the bigger bowl of paste to make the dressing; cover and refrigerate until needed.

2. Fire up the grill, bringing the temperature to high (1 to 2 seconds with the hand test). Oil the cooking grate.

3. Gently massage the 3 tablespoons of reserved paste equally over the delicate crabs, getting it in and around all of their nooks and crannies. Place the crabs on a platter, cover, and let sit at room temperature for about 15 minutes.

4. Transfer the crabs to the grate, undersides down. Grill, uncovered, for 1½ to 2 minutes, until the bodies and legs turn a deep, dusky red and opaque white. The crab bodies are full of moisture, so watch out for a little popping while they cook. Carefully flip the crabs over, brushing a bit more oil on the grate if you get any sticking at all. Grill the crabs for another 1½ to 2 minutes, keeping a close watch on them. The legs should get dark and crunchy but not black, and the bodies should have a crispy, burnished red surface but still be very moist.

5. In a large bowl, quickly toss the romaine and cabbage with enough dressing to coat them well. Spoon the greens onto individual plates and top each with a crab. Scatter scallions and avocado over the salad and serve immediately, passing the remaining dressing at the table. Every bit of the succulent soft-shells is edible.

crispy burnished crab over a tumble of cool greens

VEGETABLE MAIN AND SIDE DISHES

86

SUMMER VEGETABLE PLATTER

At the peak of summer garden goodness, this vegetable medley makes a great main course for four people or a satisfying side for a full table of diners. Serve it hot off the grill or put it in the refrigerator for a chilling treat on a warm evening. It comes with a round of goat cheese, wrapped in grape leaves to shield it from the fire. Use the recipe as a guide, adding more zucchini, less eggplant, or a different kind of pepper, depending on your garden or market and your whims. If you find the flavor of fresh oregano a bit strong, marjoram is another good herb for the accompanying dressing. **SERVES 4 AS A MAIN DISH OR 6 TO 8 AS A SIDE DISH**

FRESH OREGANO DRESSING

1/2 cup extra-virgin olive oil

2 tablespoons red or white wine vinegar, or more to taste

2 tablespoons packed fresh oregano leaves, or more to taste

1 tablespoon rinsed capers

1 garlic clove, peeled

Kosher salt or coarse sea salt to taste

Freshly ground black pepper to taste

WRAPPED CHEESE

3 to 4 large grape leaves, blanched if fresh or rinsed if bottled

One 4- to 6-ounce round creamy fresh goat cheese

2 teaspoons extra-virgin olive oil

1 1/2 pounds small eggplants (such as the slim Japanese or Asian varieties) or one 1 1/2-pound globe eggplant

3/4 pound small zucchini, sliced 1/3 inch thick

4 small red-ripe plum tomatoes, halved lengthwise

2 medium-size red, orange, or yellow bell peppers, or a combination

4 small to medium-size heads endive, halved lengthwise

1 large red onion, sliced into 1/2-inch-thick rings

About 8 metal or soaked bamboo skewers (optional)

Extra-virgin olive oil

Kosher salt or coarse salt

Capers or larger caper berries, for garnish

1. In a blender, puree the dressing ingredients. Taste and add more vinegar and oregano, if you wish. (The dressing can be made up to several hours ahead; cover and refrigerate.)

2. Fire up the grill, bringing the temperature to medium (4 to 5 seconds with the hand test).

3. Arrange the grape leaves more or less in a circle, overlapping the leaves enough to cover any holes. You want a solid wrapper of leaves. Place the cheese in the center of the leaves. Pour 1 teaspoon of the oil over the cheese and bring the leaves up over it, covering the cheese completely. The leaves will adhere to the cheese. Coat the leaves with the remaining 1 teaspoon oil. Set aside while you prepare the vegetables.

4. Peel the eggplant, but leave strips of the skin on at intervals to provide a little color contrast. Cut the eggplant into 1/3-inch-thick slices, vertical for long slender eggplants or in rounds for more corpulent eggplants. If you wish, run a skewer through each onion slice to hold the rings together while cooking. Coat all of the vegetables with oil, rubbing the eggplant most heavily. Sprinkle all with salt to taste.

5. Transfer the vegetables to the grill, in batches if necessary. When arranging the tomatoes, start them cut sides down. Grill the vegetables, uncovered, until tender, 6 to 8 minutes for the tomatoes and zucchini, 8 to 12 minutes for the eggplant and endive, 12 to 15 minutes for the peppers, and 15 to 18 minutes for the onion. Turn the peppers on each side to cook evenly and the rest of the vegetables at least once, brushing with additional oil if any appear dry.

6. Place the wrapped cheese on the grill about the time you take off the eggplant and endive. Grill the cheese for 6 to 8 minutes, turning once, until soft but short of oozing out of the protective wrap of semi-charred leaves.

7. Transfer the peppers to a plastic or paper bag and close it to let them steam, loosening the skin. When cool enough to handle, pull off any loose charred pieces of skin. Slice the peppers into thin strips, discarding the stems and seeds.

8. If you're serving the vegetables hot, fold the grape leaves back from the top of the cheese and place it in the center of a platter. If you're serving the vegetables chilled, refrigerate the cheese as well, but let it soften at room temperature before placing it on the platter. Arrange the vegetables attractively around the cheese and drizzle the dressing over all. Scatter the capers over the platter and serve.

GRILLING THE GARDEN

We've been known to fire up the grill to cook vegetables as a side dish for a nongrilled main course, particularly pasta, but not everyone may share our passion. We've tried to keep that in mind in this chapter, developing recipes that can stand on their own as an entrée or get cooked when the grill's already going for a more conventional main dish. Some of the choices make fine center-pieces for a light meal. Especially during the peak of the growing season, we're always happy with a dinner featuring one of the mixed vegetable platters, or hearty preparations such as Glistening Eggplant with Fresh Tomato Relish (page 212). If your grate space is adequate, you can also grill any of our dishes alongside an entrée that cooks at the same temperature. Since most vegetables grill best over a medium fire, they nestle cozily with chicken and pork, which usually like the same heat, and also cook well on the lower end of the two-level fires we use for burgers, steaks, and tuna.

If your grate space is too limited for that approach, grill the veggies first and then follow up with the meat. Most of these dishes lose little by sitting at room temperature for an hour before eating.

GRILLED FRENCH FRIES

This grilled version of French fries may taste even better than the original. We cut the potatoes in similar-size slices, rub them with spices to promote crusting, then give them a light coat of oil. The slow, careful cooking produces spuds that are crisp on the outside and dry and fluffy inside. **SERVES 4 TO 6 AS A SIDE DISH**

DRY RUB

1 tablespoon sweet or smoked paprika

1 teaspoon coarsely ground black pepper

1 teaspoon kosher salt or coarse sea salt

1/2 teaspoon chili powder or ground cumin

4 medium to large russet baking potatoes, scrubbed

Olive oil or vegetable oil spray

Grated mild cheese, such as cheddar or Monterey Jack, at room temperature (optional)

Ketchup, mayonnaise, or a tomato-based barbecue sauce

1. Fire up the grill, bringing the temperature to medium-low (5 to 6 seconds with the hand test).

2. Combine the dry rub ingredients in a small bowl. Cut the potatoes in half lengthwise and then slice into long wedges 1/2 inch thick at their widest side. Spray the potato spears with oil and then sprinkle them generously with the dry rub.

3. If you have a mesh grill basket or small-mesh grill rack, this is a good time to use it. Oil the basket or rack and place it on the cooking grate. Grill the potatoes, uncovered, for 30 to 35 minutes, turning them every 5 to 10 minutes. The potatoes are ready when the exteriors are brown and crisp and the interiors soft and tender.

4. If you wish, sprinkle the fries with cheese as soon as they come off the grill. Serve hot with ketchup, mayonnaise, or barbecue sauce.

HEARTLAND BOUNTY PLATTER

This hearty combo is suitable as a main course, especially with the optional sausages, or as a side dish without. On the side it works particularly well with steaks, burgers, and pork tenderloin. **SERVES 4 AS A MAIN DISH OR 6 TO 8 AS A SIDE DISH**

6 red-skinned potatoes or other small potatoes (3 to 4 ounces each), scrubbed and halved

1 large red onion, cut into 6 to 8 wedges

1 large white onion, cut into 6 to 8 wedges

6 ears corn, husks and silk removed, halved crosswise

1/2 pound yellow summer squash, sliced lengthwise into 1/3- to 1/2-inch-thick planks

8 tablespoons (1 stick) unsalted butter, melted

4 uncooked bratwursts or other uncooked sausages (about 4 ounces each; optional)

Flaky sea salt (such as Maldon), kosher salt, or coarse sea salt

Minced fresh chives, for garnish (optional)

1. Parboil the potatoes in salted water until just tender, about 10 minutes, and drain them. Run a toothpick through each onion wedge to hold it together. Brush all of the vegetables with the melted butter, using about half of it.

2. Fire up the grill, bringing the temperature to medium (4 to 5 seconds with the hand test).

3. Grill the vegetables and optional sausages, in batches if necessary. Plan on grilling times of 6 to 8 minutes for the potatoes and summer squash, 12 to 15 minutes for the onion wedges, and 20 to 25 minutes for the corn and sausages. Turn the corn and sausages on all sides to cook evenly. Turn the other vegetables three times, brushing

all of them with the remaining butter as they cook. Cook the potatoes until nicely browned on all surfaces and the rest of the vegetables until tender, removing each as it is done.

4. Arrange the vegetables and optional sausages attractively on a platter. Serve while the corn is still hot. Just before serving, sprinkle the platter with chives if you wish.

GRILLING TIP

Give the platter another flavor accent by rubbing all of the vegetables with a favorite dry rub or spice blend, perhaps something herbal or chile-based. Add the rub to taste after you've brushed everything with butter, skipping the salt unless your blend is salt-free.

SIMPLY SUPERB CORN ON THE COB

We used to grill corn on the cob in the most common traditional way, soaking the ears in water and cooking them with the husks on. By the time we were writing *Born to Grill* (Harvard Common Press, 1998), we realized that this favored method actually steams and roasts the corn, instead of grilling it, producing a good result but little true grill taste. Now we remove the husk and silk before cooking, exposing the kernels directly to the heat, which sizzles surface juices and concentrates the corn flavor. Try it and you'll quickly see the difference.

SERVES 4 AS A SIDE DISH

Unsalted butter (preferably a premium butter), melted, or mayonnaise

4 ears corn, husks and silk removed

Kosher salt or coarse sea salt (optional)

Your favorite dry rub (optional)

Finely minced fresh flat-leaf parsley or cilantro or a crumbly, somewhat dry cheese such as Cotija, Romano, or dry Jack (optional)

1. Fire up the grill, bringing the temperature to medium (4 to 5 seconds with the hand test).

2. Brush butter or mayonnaise lightly on the corn. Grill, uncovered, for about 20 minutes, turning on all sides to cook evenly and brushing with more butter after about 10 minutes. The cooking time is longer than technically necessary to cook the corn, but it helps concentrate the juices a bit, giving the corn a more intense taste and a few charred kernels.

3. Brush the corn again with butter, sprinkle it with salt or dry rub, and serve hot. If you can't resist the urge to add a little something extra, scatter on one of the herbs or a sprinkling of cheese.

GRILLING TIP

While we no longer soak corn in the husks before grilling, we occasionally soak husked ears if the corn didn't come from a farmers' market that day. Bathing the ears in water for 10 minutes helps keep the kernels from parching on the grill.

remove the husk and silk before cooking, exposing the kernels directly to the heat to sizzle juices and concentrate the corn flavor

GRILLED ONION RINGS

In a similar fashion to potatoes, you can also grill onion rings instead of frying them. The balsamic-soy marinade accentuates the caramelized flavor from the flames, without adding an identifiable Italian or Asian flavor. Experienced grillers will probably be comfortable cooking the onions directly on a well-oiled cooking grate. However, running soaked bamboo skewers through the slices or putting them in a grill basket makes the cooking even easier, keeping the onions together when you flip them. **SERVES 4 TO 6 AS A SIDE DISH**

BALSAMIC-SOY MARINADE

1/4 cup inexpensive balsamic vinegar

1 1/2 tablespoons soy sauce

1 1/2 tablespoons vegetable oil

1 large red onion, sliced into 1/3-inch-thick rings

1 large sweet onion (such as Vidalia, Maui, or Texas 1015), sliced into 1/3-inch-thick rings

About 16 metal or soaked bamboo skewers (optional)

Minced fresh chives, for garnish

1. Combine the marinade ingredients in a small bowl. If you want to hold the rings together with skewers, run one horizontally through each slice. Place the onion rings (whether skewered or not) in a large plastic bag or shallow bowl, pour the marinade over them, and let them sit at room temperature for about 30 minutes, turning occasionally.

2. Fire up the grill, bringing the temperature to medium-low (5 to 6 seconds with the hand test).

3. You can grill the onion rings directly on the cooking grate, if skewered, or arrange the slices in a well-oiled grill basket. Grill, uncovered, for 18 to 20 minutes, turning to

face the fire twice on each side and rotating a half turn each time for crisscross grill marks. The onions are ready when very soft with browned edges.

4. Arrange the onion rings on a platter, sprinkle with chives for a bit of color, and serve hot or at room temperature.

the balsamic-soy marinade accentuates the caramelized flavor from the flames, without adding an identifiable Italian or Asian flavor

GLISTENING EGGPLANT WITH FRESH TOMATO RELISH

We marinate and baste this eggplant to make it shine in all ways, and then serve it with a lusty red and white relish of good, ripe tomatoes and silky mozzarella cheese. If you're not trying for a strictly vegetarian dish, a sprinkling of crumbled bacon is a scrumptious addition. **SERVES 4 AS A MAIN DISH OR 6 TO 8 AS A SIDE DISH**

Two 1-pound globe eggplants, peeled and cut lengthwise into 1/3- to 1/2-inch-thick slices

MARINADE AND BASTE

1/2 cup extra-virgin olive oil

2 tablespoons rice vinegar

2 tablespoons minced fresh thyme or 1 tablespoon dried crumbled thyme

1 teaspoon crushed red pepper (optional)

1/2 teaspoon kosher salt or coarse sea salt

FRESH TOMATO RELISH

2 cups halved tiny tomatoes, such as pear, Sweet 100, or cherry, preferably red and yellow

3 ounces fresh mozzarella, preferably water-packed, cut into small cubes

1 tablespoon top-quality extra-virgin olive oil

Scant 1 teaspoon rice vinegar

1/4 teaspoon kosher salt or coarse sea salt, or more to taste

Generous grinding of black pepper

1. Whisk together the marinade ingredients in a small bowl. Place the eggplant slices on a baking sheet. Brush the marinade over both sides of the slices, and let sit at room temperature for 15 to 30 minutes.

2. Combine the relish ingredients in a medium-size bowl and set aside.

3. Fire up the grill, bringing the temperature to medium (4 to 5 seconds with the hand test).

4. Drain the eggplant, reserving any marinade not absorbed by the thirsty vegetable.

5. Grill, uncovered, for 10 to 12 minutes, turning the slices to face the fire twice on both sides and rotating a half turn each time for crisscross grill marks. About halfway through the cooking, brush the eggplant with the reserved marinade. The slices are ready when soft and juicy.

6. Arrange the eggplant slices, overlapping, on a platter. Serve hot or at room temperature, with the relish spooned on top.

marinate and baste this eggplant to make it shine in all ways, and then serve it with a lusty relish of good, ripe tomatoes and silky mozzarella cheese

ASPARAGUS WITH LEMON-BACON VINAIGRETTE

You can cook asparagus in a variety of ways, but to us, no other cooking method beats grilling. Put the result together with an updated version of an old-fashioned bacon vinaigrette and you've got a splendid side for almost any main course. This should be a top-100 grill dish on everybody's list of favorites.

SERVES 4 AS A SIDE DISH

LEMON-BACON VINAIGRETTE

2 slices bacon, chopped

3 tablespoons extra-virgin olive oil

1 to 1 1/2 tablespoons fresh lemon juice

1/4 teaspoon sugar

1/4 teaspoon kosher salt or coarse sea salt

1 to 1 1/4 pounds asparagus spears, preferably pencil-thin, woody ends trimmed

1. To prepare the vinaigrette, first fry the bacon in a skillet over medium heat until crisp. Drain the bacon with a slotted spoon and crumble it, reserving both the bacon and the drippings. Remove the skillet from the heat, but while still hot, whisk the oil, 1 tablespoon of the lemon juice, the sugar, and salt into the bacon drippings. Taste and add the remaining 1/2 tablespoon lemon juice if needed to balance the dressing.

2. Spoon out 2 to 3 teaspoons of the dressing and rub it evenly over the asparagus.

3. Fire up the grill, bringing the temperature to medium (4 to 5 seconds with the hand test).

4. Transfer the asparagus to the grill, placing them perpendicular to the bars of the grate, with the stem ends over the hottest part of the fire and the tips out toward

a cooler edge. Grill, uncovered, until tender, 5 to 6 minutes for thin spears or 6 to 8 minutes for thicker spears, rolling the asparagus frequently to cook on all sides.

5. Serve the asparagus hot or chilled on a long platter, with the remaining vinaigrette drizzled over it and the crumbled bacon scattered over the top.

a top-100 grill dish on everybody's list of favorites

S'MORES
AND
MORE FOR
DESSERT

HOT BANANA SPLIT

If you serve this to friends once, they'll beg for it every time they return. You just warm the bananas on the grill (don't char them) to soften the texture and mellow the flavor, making them more receptive than ever to a cool ice cream topping. **SERVES 4 VERY GENEROUSLY**

1 cup sugar

1/2 cup half-and-half

6 tablespoons (3/4 stick) unsalted butter

4 medium-size bananas

Three 1.4-ounce Heath bars or 4 to 5 ounces chocolate-covered toffee, chopped into chunks

4 large scoops each of two kinds of ice cream, such as vanilla, butter pecan, praline, chocolate, or banana

Whipped cream

Toasted almonds, for garnish

1. Fire up the grill, bringing the temperature to medium (4 to 5 seconds with the hand test). Oil the cooking grate.

2. Combine the sugar and half-and-half in a medium-size heavy saucepan. Bring the mixture to a full rolling boil, stirring occasionally. Stir in the butter until melted and remove from the heat.

3. Just before grilling, slice the bananas, still in their skins, lengthwise.

4. Transfer the bananas, cut sides down, to the grate. Grill, uncovered, for 3 to 4 minutes. Turn the bananas skin sides down, brush their cut surfaces with a few teaspoons of the half-and-half mixture, and grill them for another 2 to 3 minutes, until soft and lightly colored.

5. Remove the bananas from their skins. If you own long banana split dishes, leave the banana halves whole and place two of them in each dish. If not, cut the bananas into bite-size chunks and divide them among individual serving dishes.

6. Return the half-and-half mixture to medium-low heat and stir in the toffee chunks. Cook briefly until the chocolate and toffee have partially melted (leaving some chunkiness) and stir well.

7. Top each dish of banana with one scoop of each ice cream and some of the chocolate-toffee sauce. Add whipped cream, top with almonds, and serve immediately.

A FRUITFUL FINISH

Most of the recipes in this chapter highlight fruit fancied up in some respect. Warming fruit over the grill caramelizes sugar on the surface, softens texture, and releases sweet juices, producing a toasty, natural wrap-up for a meal. With the addition of complementary flavors—such as brown sugar, honey, ginger, and cinnamon—you can elaborate the dimensions into a full-fledged dessert. For total extravagance, all that's lacking is ice cream.

We've designed the fruit desserts so that much—and sometimes all—of the prep work can be done prior to dinner, leaving just the final cooking until the end. If you're grilling other parts of the meal as well, think through your strategy in advance. With a gas grill, it's easy enough to shut down after the main course and then fire up again when you're ready for dessert. When you're cooking with charcoal, try to time your dinner to keep the fire going at a low level warm enough for a second round of cooking.

GOOEY GOOD S'MORES

This old treat, which the Girl Scouts started popularizing in 1927, retains all of its childhood appeal, even for the most mature campfire fans. The basic combo is flawless, but that doesn't mean you can't improvise occasionally. Add a smear of peanut butter, trade out milk chocolate for white chocolate, or plate the finished s'mores and drizzle with a little fruit sauce. Always serve with plenty of napkins and either a tall, frosty glass of milk or maybe a snifter of Cognac.

SERVES 1

> 1 large marshmallow
>
> 2 graham cracker squares
>
> 3/4 ounce milk chocolate or semisweet chocolate, in a flat square (1/2 the popular-size Hershey Bar), or chips

1. Fire up the grill, bringing the temperature to medium-low (5 to 6 seconds with the hand test).

2. Thread the marshmallow on a skewer, long fork, section of a coat hanger, or even a smooth stick. Place the graham crackers on the cooking grate. Hold the marshmallow a couple of inches above the grate and toast it on all sides for several minutes, until very soft and golden.

3. While the marshmallow toasts, turn the graham crackers, place the chocolate on one of them, and continue heating the crackers until the marshmallow is ready. Top the chocolate with the marshmallow and the second cracker. Grill for an additional minute or two, turning again if the bottom is browning deeply. Multiply the recipe as needed.

PIÑA COLADA PINEAPPLE SPEARS

With its especially high sugar content, pineapple's a natural for the grill, as long as you don't torch it. If you like piña colada cocktails, or just want to dream about being in the tropics, this is the dessert for you. **SERVES 4**

> 1 medium-size pineapple or one 20-ounce container unsliced fresh pineapple
>
> **MARINADE**
>
> 1/3 cup dark rum, preferably, or light rum
>
> Juice of 1 medium-size lime
>
> 2 tablespoons canned cream of coconut
>
> 1/2 teaspoon ground mace or nutmeg
>
> Lime slices, for garnish

1. Fire up the grill, bringing the temperature to medium (4 to 5 seconds with the hand test).

2. If you have a whole pineapple, slice off the top and reserve it for garnishing the plate. Cut off a small slice at the bottom so it can stand evenly and then cut off all of the pineapple skin, slicing only as deeply as needed to remove the tiny brown eyes. Halve the pineapple lengthwise and then cut each half into long 1-inch-thick spears. Cut away the tough fibrous core side of each spear. If working with already skinned pineapple, simply cut it into spears.

3. Place the pineapple in a zipper-top plastic bag or shallow dish. Combine the marinade ingredients in a small bowl and pour the mixture over the pineapple. Let it sit at room temperature for 30 to 60 minutes.

4. Drain the pineapple spears, discarding the marinade. Transfer the spears to the cooking grate and grill, uncovered, for 5 to 6 minutes, turning on all sides, until soft with browned edges. Serve immediately, garnished with the lime slices.

GRILLED PEACHES WITH GORGONZOLA

Cheese with fruit makes a sophisticated finish to a fine meal. The combination of a creamy rich Gorgonzola or other blue cheese with naturally sweet summer peaches kissed by the fire is about as simple yet special as a dessert can be.
SERVES 4 OR MORE

> 2 pounds firm but ripe peaches, peeled, pitted, and halved
>
> Vegetable oil spray
>
> 4 ounces Gorgonzola or other creamy rich blue cheese, crumbled, at room temperature

1. Fire up the grill, bringing the temperature to medium (4 to 5 seconds with the hand test).

2. Spritz the peaches lightly with oil and transfer to the cooking grate, cut sides down. Grill, uncovered, for 6 to 8 minutes, or as needed, turning once, until softened with a few brown and caramelized edges.

3. Divide among bowls, sprinkle immediately with the cheese so that it softens, and serve warm.

HONEYED FIGS

These taste wonderful with any type of honey, from mild orange-blossom to a deeply flavored variety such as lavender honey. **SERVES 4 OR MORE**

1/3 cup honey

1 tablespoon hot water

12 fresh figs, halved lengthwise

Vegetable oil spray

1. Fire up the grill, bringing the temperature to medium (4 to 5 seconds with the hand test).

2. Whisk together the honey and hot water in a small bowl.

3. Dip the cut side of each fig into the honey.

4. Spritz the figs with oil and transfer to the cooking grate, cut sides down. Grill, uncovered, for 5 to 7 minutes, turning once and brushing if you wish with any remaining honey. The figs are ready when soft and oozing juice.

GRILLING TIP

We can think of scores of ways to enjoy these—or any—figs. Place them warm over vanilla or rum-raisin ice cream or beside a couple of small rounds of goat cheese, a spoonful of ricotta, or a small wedge of blue cheese. Sprinkle with chopped fresh mint or lemon thyme. Grill tangerine or orange wedges alongside the figs until soft with a few charred edges and serve them together.

APPLE WEDGES WITH WHISKEY-CARAMEL SAUCE

Basted with a high-octane, made-for-grownups caramel sauce, these apples won't be found at a state fair booth. Sweet, smoky, and crunchy, they make a fine wrap to any outdoor evening. If you like French-inspired salted caramel, sprinkle these at the end with flakes of *fleur de sel* or Maldon sea salt. **SERVES 4**

WHISKEY CARAMEL SAUCE

4 tablespoons ($1/2$ stick) unsalted butter

$3/4$ cup packed brown sugar

$1/4$ teaspoon ground cinnamon

$1/4$ cup whiskey or bourbon

$1/4$ cup whipping cream

4 medium-size apples

Metal or soaked bamboo skewers (optional)

4 tablespoons ($1/2$ stick) unsalted butter, melted

Fleur de sel or Maldon sea salt (optional)

1. To prepare the caramel sauce, first combine the butter, brown sugar, cinnamon, and bourbon in a small, heavy saucepan. Bring the mixture to a boil over medium heat and boil for 2 minutes, stirring frequently. Remove the syrup from the heat and stir in the cream, watching out for sputtering steam. (The sauce can be made to this point a week or more ahead, covered, and stored in the refrigerator. Reheat it gently before proceeding, adding a little water if it seems too stiff to drizzle after heating.)

2. Fire up the grill, bringing the temperature to medium (4 to 5 seconds with the hand test).

3. Peel and core the apples, cutting each into 1-inch thick wedges. Thread the apples onto skewers or lay them on a well-oiled small-mesh grill rack. Brush the apples with the melted butter.

4. Transfer the skewers to the cooking grate and grill, uncovered, for 10 to 12 minutes, turning at least once, until the apples are tender. In the last 1 to 2 minutes of cooking, baste with about two-thirds of the caramel sauce.

5. Divide the apples among individual serving bowls. Drizzle with the remaining sauce, sprinkle with salt, if you wish, and serve immediately.

sweet, smoky, and crunchy, they make a fine wrap to any outdoor evening

KALEIDOSCOPE FRUIT KEBOBS

Any soft-textured fruit works for these dessert skewers, but they're most appealing with a varied range of colors. Brush with some honey butter and you've got a perfect fruit finish. **SERVES 4**

> 1¹/2 pounds mixed soft-textured fruit chunks, such as mango or pineapple chunks; peeled peach quarters; halved, pitted plums, nectarines, or apricots; whole strawberries, whole pitted sweet cherries; melon balls; peel-on tangerine quarters; or thick slices of peeled kiwi
>
> Metal or soaked bamboo skewers, preferably 2 for each kebob
>
> **HONEY BUTTER**
>
> ¹/4 cup honey
>
> 2 tablespoons unsalted butter
>
> 1 tablespoon water
>
> Minced fresh mint (optional)

1. Fire up the grill, bringing the temperature to medium (4 to 5 seconds with the hand test). Oil the cooking grate.

2. Thread the fruit chunks on skewers in alternating colors, preferably using 2 parallel skewers per kebob to hold the ingredients securely while cooking. Push the fruit together to touch but not squash the neighboring fruit.

3. Combine the honey butter ingredients in a small saucepan over medium heat. Stir to combine. Brush the kebobs lightly with the honey butter.

4. Transfer the kebobs to the grate. Grill, uncovered, for 7 to 10 minutes, turning on all sides, until the fruits are softened and a few edges are browned. Brush the kebobs thickly with the honey butter in the last couple of minutes of cooking.

5. Serve the kebobs hot, sprinkled with mint, if you wish.

CRUNCHY CARAMELIZED PEARS

Fruit on the grill caramelizes naturally, but we rev up the effect here with a brown-sugar bath. The addition of toasty walnut oil and slightly astringent walnuts keeps the sweetness in balance. **SERVES 4**

> 4 ripe medium-size pears, peeled, halved, and cored
>
> 1/4 cup walnut oil
>
> 1/4 cup packed brown sugar, preferably dark
>
> Toasted walnut pieces, for garnish

1. Fire up the grill, bringing the temperature to medium (4 to 5 seconds with the hand test).

2. Place the pears in a shallow dish. Pour the oil over them and turn to coat evenly. Sprinkle the pears with the brown sugar and let them sit for about 15 minutes. Drain the pears, reserving the oil-sugar mixture.

3. Transfer the pears to the cooking grate, cut sides down. Grill, uncovered, for 8 to 10 minutes, turning once. The pears are ready when softened, with a few browned edges.

4. Drizzle a little of the remaining oil-sugar mixture into the pears' cavities, sprinkle them with walnuts, and serve warm.

MEASUREMENT EQUIVALENTS

PLEASE NOTE THAT ALL CONVERSIONS ARE APPROXIMATE.

LIQUID CONVERSIONS

U.S.	METRIC
1 tsp	5 ml
1 tbs	15 ml
2 tbs	30 ml
3 tbs	45 ml
1/4 cup	60 ml
1/3 cup	75 ml
1/3 cup + 1 tbs	90 ml
1/3 cup + 2 tbs	100 ml
1/2 cup	120 ml
2/3 cup	150 ml
3/4 cup	180 ml
3/4 cup + 2 tbs	200 ml
1 cup	240 ml
1 cup + 2 tbs	275 ml
1 1/4 cups	300 ml
1 1/3 cups	325 ml
1 1/2 cups	350 ml
1 2/3 cups	375 ml
1 3/4 cups	400 ml
1 3/4 cups + 2 tbs	450 ml
2 cups (1 pint)	475 ml
2 1/2 cups	600 ml
3 cups	720 ml
4 cups (1 quart)	945 ml (1,000 ml is 1 liter)

WEIGHT CONVERSIONS

U.S./U.K.	METRIC
1/2 oz	14 g
1 oz	28 g
1 1/2 oz	43 g
2 oz	57 g
2 1/2 oz	71 g
3 oz	85 g
3 1/2 oz	100 g
4 oz	113 g
5 oz	142 g
6 oz	170 g
7 oz	200 g
8 oz	227 g
9 oz	255 g
10 oz	284 g
11 oz	312 g
12 oz	340 g
13 oz	368 g
14 oz	400 g
15 oz	425 g
1 lb	454 g

OVEN TEMPERATURE CONVERSIONS

°F	GAS MARK	°C
250	1/2	120
275	1	140
300	2	150
325	3	165
350	4	180
375	5	190
400	6	200
425	7	220
450	8	230
475	9	240
500	10	260
550	Broil	290

INDEX

Asparagus with Lemon-
    Bacon Vinaigrette,
    214–15
Avocados
    Drunken Fajitas, 82–83
    Soft-Shell Crab Salad,
    198–99

B

Bacon
    Figs, and Charred Onions,
        Pork Tenderloin Filled
        with, 113–14
    -Lemon Vinaigrette, 214
    Lobster BLT, 196–97
Balsamic-Soy Marinade, 210
Banana Split, Hot, 218–19
Barbecue butter, preparing,
    13
Barbecued Chicken Breasts,
    Bodacious, 126–27
Barbecued Shrimp,
    Louisiana, 186–87
Barbecue Sauce, 126–27
    Dr Pepper, 115–16
    flavor variations, 128
Basil
    Classic Italian Pizza with
        Fire-Roasted Tomato
        Sauce, 34–35
    Oil, 168
    -Scented Salmon, 168–69
Beef
    All-American Backyard
        Burgers, 56–57
    Berghoff's Chicago Beer
        Burgers, 58–60
    bone-in rib-eye, about,
        101
    Caribbean Curry Burgers,
        61–62
    Carpetbag Steak, 98
    Chuck Steak Tacos, 86–87

Cumin-Rubbed Carne
    Asada, 84–85
Doggone Good Hot Dog,
    71
Drunken Fajitas, 82–83
Florentine T-Bone, 102
grilling thick steaks, tips
    for, 97
grinding, for burgers, 60
Lettuce Wraps with Asian
    Steak, 26–27
origins of Salisbury steak,
    57
Pickapeppa-Marinated
    Flank Steak, 104–5
A Porterhouse from
    Heaven, 96
steaks, in Colonial
    America, 105
Stephan Pyles' Texas Rib-
    Eye, 99–101
Texas Fajitas, 78–80
Beer
    -Braised Onions, 58–59
    Bratwurst Roll,
        Sheboygan-Style,
        72–73
    Brew Marinade, 72–73
    Marinade, 82
    -Mushroom Ketchup,
        58–59
Berghoff's Chicago Beer
    Burgers, 58–60
Bison
    Burgers, Great Plains,
        63–64
    Steak, Mustard-Rubbed,
        103
Blue Corn and Green Chile
    Pizza, 50–52
Bodacious Barbecued
    Chicken Breasts,
    126–27

Bratwurst Roll, Sheboygan-
    Style, 72–73
Bread crumbs, 193
Bread. See also Pizza
    Fired Onion Flatbread,
        48–49
    Grilled Cheese Sandwich
        on a Stick, 28
    Speared Chicken Caesar
        Salad, 18–19
Brew Marinade, 72–73
Burgers
    All-American Backyard,
        56–57
    Berghoff's Chicago Beer,
        58–60
    Bison, Great Plains,
        63–64
    Caribbean Curry,
        61–62
    Lamb, Rosemary and
        Mint, 65
    Portobello, 68–69
    Tuna, Pacific Rim, 70
    Turkey, Herb-Rubbed,
        66–67
Butter
    barbecue, preparing, 13
    Honey, 226
    Smoked Salmon, 177
Buttery Heritage Turkey,
    154–55

C

Cabbage
    Soft-Shell Crab Salad,
        198–99
Caesar Dressing, 18–19
Caesar Salad, Chicken,
    Speared, 18–19
Capers
    Hot and Cool Pizza, 40–41
    topping pizza with, 37